Music Journalism 101

The definitive resource for new and established writers.

Leticia Supple

DEDICATION

This work is dedicated to all of the writers and photographers worldwide with whom I have been privileged to work, and to all those who keep the metal spirit alive. Many thanks, and much love to you all.

PREFACE

Welcome to the long-promised Music Journalism 101 in book form.

For many years, this book has been "in the works". For the same amount of time, I have avoided approaching what I feared would be a mammoth task. My ability to procrastinate is of superhuman proportions.

Having been mentoring writers—young and old—and having had young, excited journos asking repeatedly for the book, I finally decided that enough procrastination was enough. I started planning. Once I planned, I could write. No surprises there. It's how I've always worked.

The original Music Journalism 101 that I wrote, and posted progressively on my blog, was by all accounts the first of its kind online. This book appears to also be the only one of its kind, at least in the depth and coverage that it provides.

Over the years I've added to the knowledge base, written adjunct essays, collaborated on other things, developed quick reference guides, and generally expanded my point of view.

Thus, this book version is updated and expanded. May you find it useful, helpful, and worth coming back to in years to come.

In doing so, please join in my gratitude to the various writers, photographers, and publicists who have provided feedback, encouragement, and assistance over the years. Without them, this book would never have been possible.

Enjoy!

~ Leticia, Adelaide, 2012-13

CONTENTS

INTRODUCTION

by Tom Valcanis

Why music criticism? Lillian Roxon did it because she wanted to be the "Mother of Rock." Lester Bangs did it because he believed himself a conduit to understanding the music as much as a guitar or voice was to creating it. Everett True does it because he wanted to tell people what tunes made him dance, and why. Charlie Gillett simply did it for the free promo LPs, keeping the ones he wanted and selling the ones he didn't.

Music journalism and criticism as a field has never been fully structured or stratified by industry or academia. Unlike general news or sports journalism, there are scant notions of orthodoxy or proper procedure as handed down from lecturers or respected practitioners on high, preserving the traditions carved in stone by Syme or Hearst or Pulitzer. You can buy countless volumes penned by Robert Christgau, Greil Marcus or Simon Frith, marvelling at their stellar prose and unflinchingly bold copy but as far as music journalism or criticism is concerned, that is the territory. There's no map to follow to create your own.

You can run library searches on "criticism—literary" or "criticism—film" and occasionally turn up rock n' roll hagiographies of your favorite martyr who has bravely fallen in the service of rock writing. Rarer still are narrative histories of music criticism itself. Frustrated, you may turn to the journalism section where you'll find tomes dedicated to structuring copy and "how to report" as a journalist, but insofar music criticism is concerned, there's nothing instructional on the shelves.

Having written an exhaustive thesis on the subject myself (to which I owe Leticia a debt of gratitude for her invaluable assistance), I have trawled the literature for comparable works. To my knowledge, there exists no book to my knowledge that covers the depth and probity of Leticia's work on the mechanics of rock music criticism; certainly not one that acutely defines the major areas of criticism from record reviews, live reports and the coveted rock star interview. Thousands upon thousands of words are heaped upon another to hammer out a theory as to why *Pitchfork.com* or *Rolling Stone* are respected voices/unit pushers, but not *how*.

In an unwieldy transition phase from music press being the gatekeepers and tastemakers, toward lending a voice to the overall "conversation" (or an anachronistic irrelevance at worst), a guiding hand in the right direction to aid budding music writers is sorely needed. This more so than ever in critical music journalism's storied history.

Whether rock journalism and criticism toils in service of publicists or not, an obligation to professional conduct and practice must continue uninterrupted.

The honey pot of music journalism was never sticky with cash. In today's age, where exemplars of the craft are forced to drive cabs or wait tables to make a living, it need not mean that the quality or professionalism expected of all journalists dips below an acceptable standard.

We need new blood pumping around the ossified arteries of music journalism. The cult of Jann Wenner and *NME* have had a stranglehold on the international rock journalism field since 1967; we need a new generation to go rogue, to pen iconoclastic stories in defence of the new, and to spark a contemporary rock writing revolution.

Precisely this book will serve as a starting point. It is for fans of music that are compelled by that need to write, and to add their analyses and interpretations of why the music matters or does not. Instead of leaving writers to carbon copy others and hope for the best, Leticia's introductory course on music journalism will provide the tools necessary for new writers to forge their own paths, without the burdensome load of academia or the "establishment" incumbent upon them.

To the music writers of the future—rock on; you're in good hands.

~ Tom Valcanis, Melbourne, 2012

Tom Valcanis is a freelance music journalist and critic who resides in Melbourne, Australia. He was one of the first writers to join Leticia's Metalasfuck.net team in 2009. He completed a Master's thesis on contemporary rock journalism in Australia in 2011. Since, he has professionally written music journalism for The Big Issue, TheVine.com.au and Australian Hysteria Magazine.

1. GOOD FOUNDATIONS: A BIT ABOUT ETHNOGRAPHY

Ethnography[1] is properly from the science of anthropology. In relatively recent years, the practice of ethnography has grown well beyond its original uses. These days, ethnographers are not just academics and researchers, but also essayists and nonfiction writers: people who go out into uncomfortable or odd situations and then write about their experiences afterwards. Others work in organisational communication[2], participating in a culture, writing about it, analysing it, to see how it could be improved and how knowledge can best be retained and used. Still others are in marketing—and there's a whole field of enthography online now too (it's called netnography[3], where the focus is on online communities).

One of the primary focuses of ethnography is on analysis through story, pattern recognition, and the awfully worded but reasonably apt notion of 'transformation of the self'. The idea with the latter is that as an ethnographer, you can participate in an event (or community, or organisation) and that you will not be the same when you come out, as when you went in.

Ethnography is also self-reflexive practice. That is, it's a style of work where you are continually reflecting on what you're doing. You reflect on your own participation, on your own reactions to things, on your own style of being within that community. Even if such reflexivity is not written down formally, ethnographers use the reflection when they're writing their work; it creates a rich, textured fabric of prose, such that the reader gets an instant, real sense of place, people, and times. Without any other marker posts, the reader instinctively knows that the account is faithful to the experience.

At the same time, reflexivity allows the ethnographer to write him- or herself into the piece. This results in a piece of work that is not distant or seemingly 'unauthored', and gives the writing a sense of someone having been there, whether or not the reflective notions are written in.

In some ways, one could potentially approach music journalism— particularly when one is covering events—as though one might approach a 'text' in the sense that Fairclough might have[4]. This would mean that a gig as a whole would be one 'text', the beer garden might be a 'text' within that one, and so on. One might feel inclined to examine the interaction observed between people's roles, between texts, contexts, subtexts, and so on.

There have been various anthropological documentaries[5] in the past few years that evaluate the culture and the notions behind the metal scene, but that is a whole separate issue, and one that is not relevant for the purposes of Music Journalism 101.

It is with the so-called 'new' ethnographies[6] that we are concerned here. The 'new' ethnographies are creative narratives, focused more on the writer's experience than on a particular culture. In terms of music journalism, this type of ethnography is really important. The idea of 'participant observer'[7] is a key one, and the idea of being able to turn onto everything all at once and be able to get it down effectively is essential.

Lloyd Goodall put it well, when he wrote about the new ethnographies[8]:

> "Unlike other methods of inquiry and writing, simply acquiring the knowledge and applying the processes involved doesn't make you an ethnographer.

> "To become an ethnographer who writes new ethnographies requires habits of being in the world, of being able to talk and listen to people, and of being able to write—habits that are beyond method. These ethnographic practices involve a craft that anyone can learn, but there is also an art to it, a confluence made out of the person and the process, one that separates those who know about and can theorize new ethnography from those who know about, theorize about, and do it.

"It is a difference that emerges on the written page.

"Which is to say: New ethnographers are not researchers who learn how to 'write it up,' but writers who learn how to use their research and how they write to 'get it down'."

The key notion from Goodall's work is that of 'doing' ethnography. It's something you have to actively be aware of doing; it's not passive work. It takes considerable conscious effort to do it well.

Doing a 'new ethnography' in the field of metal music journalism requires the habit of being a part of the metal community, the habit of being able to talk and listen to lots of different people on a common subject (music/metal) and as a peer. But you still need to be able to write, and to have a habit of writing—and if you can do this creatively, so much the better. As a metal music journo/ethnographer, you need to be able to 'get it down' while you can, and flesh it out and create some new monster out of it when you're no longer wrapped up in that show, or this festival, or that party. Making more out of your notes requires solid observational skills and the ability to recall elements effectively: the latter comes with conscious awareness.

Of course, what underpins all of these habits is the habit of observation. It is surprising how few people really understand or see what goes on around them, and how many fewer can recall it later on. The key is to practice your observational skills.

Mark Rouncefield at Lancaster University posted a lecture online[9], available to the public, which includes notes on how to 'do' organisational ethnography. Lots of it is relevant to the present notion of ethnography as journalism and there are some excellent points he raises. With a bit of creative thought you can apply some of the principles to your own work. I highly recommend you go and read through it; you can find it online at <http://www.cs.nott.ac.uk/~tar/DBC/dbc-lecture4.pdf>.

THINGS TO PRACTICE AND KEY TASKS

TASK ONE: Practice observation without taking notes

For the time being, your key task is to practice your observational skills. It doesn't matter how or where you do this. You can do it in a park, in the supermarket, at your mate's house, at a restaurant... wherever. Take notice of everything that goes on around you. You also need to participate as normal in whatever situation you're in, without staring, without asking pointed questions; in short, you need to just do your thing.

Take notice of conversations, environment, smells, sounds... everything. Then, once you are outside the environment, write down as much of it as you can remember. Can you create a creative, interesting piece out of it? If you can write, this should be easy.

Remember to include yourself in your environment—this part is essential. Eventually, with enough practice, you'll find your observational muscles gaining strength. And you will also start to build your writing skills. Two birds for the price of one!

TASK TWO: Honing your skills—observation and note-taking

Do the same as for task one, but periodically scratch some notes to yourself. If you're out for dinner, a good way to do this is when you go to the toilet—but don't do it so often that people think you've got diarrhoea or bowel problems!†

When you get home, take your notes and what you remember, and write it up as creatively as you can.

Remember to Reflect

Working ethnographically means that you must reflect on what you are doing. This has huge benefits. If you reflect enough, you start to learn from yourself. You can explain to others what you do, and how and why. It goes back to the age-old adage that what you can measure you can improve. Reflection is a process of continuous learning.

Reflect on the process of observation and how it worked for you. What would you change, and why? What elements of the situation did you miss?

Reflect on your participation. Do you find yourself getting distant, staring, or not participating fully in the situation or interaction? What sort of reaction did you get? Did you find people changing their behaviours? What could you do about this?

Reflect on the way you write up your work. How can you turn it into an interesting, richly textured, non-fiction piece? What would you need to flesh out, what sort of different notes would you need to take?

Reflect on the reading experience. Could you give your piece to someone else and have them 'experience' the situation as well? Why or why not, and what would you need to do differently?

2. ETHNOGRAPHY AT GIGS: HOW AND WHY

Using ethnography to develop your observational skills is invaluable when it comes to gigs at which you are one of the stated journalists. For a start, especially if you're a metalhead, you are one of the many excited participants in the event. Moving on from there, you need to not only participate and (hopefully) enjoy yourself; you need to observe everything about the show, and everything about the performance, enough to recreate a good story later: one that readers will be absorbed in, so much so that they too 'experience' the gig. And, as pointed out towards the end of the last chapter, it helps you to refine your abilities in this direction.

The how and why of ethnography is important. This chapter will give you a bit of a to the ethnographic principles you can use in practise. This chapter does not cover how to write a review of bands performing on a stage in front of you, however. It covers everything surrounding that. In other words, the show itself (people, sound, lights, vibe etc.).

Hopefully you've taken a bit of time to digest the first chapter, and to practice your observational skills to learn the nuances of situations in which you find yourself. If you are serious about learning how to hone your observational skills, you will also be finding yourself able to fairly sharply recreate those situations in writing.

I am going to reiterate here that writers need to do ethnography—so if you don't write (at all), and you're attempting ethnography, it's possible that you won't gain skills to the same extent as someone who writes often.

Further to this, it is an opinion of mine—borne through long experience—that the best music writers are writers first. Hopefully they have an understanding of music, too, in any of its forms. It's bloody hard work to write about time signatures when you have not a clue what a time signature is! . So—let's dive into ethnography at gigs.

The test of your abilities is finding yourself in a gig situation and being faced with the notion of doing ethnography through the entire show. If shows you head out to are anything like the ones I get to see, then you'll find you're faced with two, sometimes three or four, support acts, plus one or two headlining acts. The entire night can go from 7 pm until 2 am, all (or at least some) of your mates are there, and everyone's drinking and having a good time. If you're a smoker, it's very possible that, like here in Australia, you're faced with the fact that you have to go outside to have a cigarette—so you have to factor that in as well.

Please note that while you can get drunk at shows that you are reviewing, it's really poor form. For start, you usually being paid to be there (if not in cash or wages, then in the cost of the ticket, which is your free entry), and someone is counting on you to do a good job. A good job, is one that is comprehensive, well written, takes into account every band on the bill, is insightful, and—if your editor is anything like me—adheres to good critical principles.

There is a huge amount of which to take account. You can't necessarily afford to be selective in regards to how much notice you take of what. You need to be like a never-ending sponge, and absorb absolutely everything you can.

If you have to take some notes when you head to the toilet, that's perfectly ok: if it helps you to recreate a show faithfully, and if it helps you to retain the textures of the night (especially if you're drinking too!) then by all means do it. I always take notes at shows; if not of the show itself, then at least of the set list of each band.

If you are reporting for a specific publication, absolutely ensure that, if you're drinking, that you don't have so much that everything gets fuzzy—because then you'll be in strife when you confront your notes the next day. Trust me, I've been there and it's not a good feeling. At best, you'll end up ringing your friends "to discuss last night's gig". At worst, you'll rely on overworked clichés, and end up fabricating whole portions of performances.

Don't laugh, very drunk colleagues at the same show have admitted to me that they do this. Try not to get yourself in this situation.

Observations of which you need to be conscious

There are a handful of things you need to pay attention to when you head out to a show. Each one is discussed below.

1. How you feel about the show, before you get there.

One of the first things, especially if you're seeing a band you particularly like, or haven't seen before, or thought you would never get to see (which happens a lot in Australia!), is how you feel about going to see it.

Writing ethnography is not about writing yourself out of the picture and concentrating on what's happening around you; remember, you are a participant in the event, so what your thoughts and feelings are count enormously towards what is going on. If you can make some notes about these things ahead of time, then you'll be in a better position to paint a more colourful picture later on.

2. Mistakes that you make.

If you are late to the show, if you miss a band, if you fuck up and get the wrong venue or the wrong time: write it all in! There is nothing more refreshing than someone who writes honestly about their participation.

And don't worry about how bands feel about you missing them. You are far better off writing that you were running late (even if you were running late on purpose; see point number one) and missed XYZ Band, than you are to ignore them altogether. At least this way the band will get some recognition, even if it's through your own error.

3. When you first get to the venue: take stock, inside and out.

Getting to the venue can sometimes be a story in itself. Imagine you had to stay back at work, you still need to get dressed, you're famished, it's pouring rain, and the show starts in fifteen minutes. Tell us the story! It sets the stage for what happens afterwards.

What's the weather like (important if there are going to be people congregating outside!)? Is there a line at the door? How many people are there? What are the staff like? Did the door staff scowl at you running in breathless with garlic on your breath and sauce in your hair? And so on.

When you get inside the venue, you are confronted with a million things at once: the state of the bar and how busy it is; the temperature—sometimes it's as hot as the depths of Hell! Where is the merch table, what sort of merchandise is available, and how popular is it? What's the beer like? What sort of vibe does the place have?

There are so many things here that you can take notice of—and to some extent you need to cover them all.

Some interesting things are only noticeable at particular shows, too. Things like, what's the male-female ratio like? For some genres, like grindcore, there is likely to be more males than females; for metalcore it might be balanced; for black metal it might be full of kvlt male metallers and female poseurs.

If you don't think this is important, stop a moment. Such things make a difference because it often affects the ways in which crowds behave. A full-on circle pit that takes up a good proportion of front-of-stage, filled with aggression and violence, is less likely to happen if there are more females than males, for example.

4. Remember that you're participating and that what you see/hear does count!

While you're taking notice of all of these things, you are hearing what people are saying. You are participating in conversations; you are drinking and/or smoking; you are getting a sense of the vibe of the show.

Which brings me to the next point: trust your instincts. If you get a bad feeling from the crowd, trust it! It's likely you'll be right, or at least that it will impact on some other element of the show.

The other warning I have to give you is this one: don't screw up your relationships and people's trust by writing their conversations into your review, unless it is humorous, relevant, or supports a point you are trying to make. You can write about how shit a band is and include comments you hear throughout the crowd if there are a lot of them. You can not include hearsay, gossip, or confidential information. Even if you don't feel like a professional, at least act like one.

5. Crowd reactions

When you actually get to seeing bands take to the stage, you'll notice how the crowd reacts—and this is vital. Keep a sharp eye on vibe indicators: bored crowds carry on conversations, go back to the bar, walk out and have a smoke, half pay attention. They might swear at the band, or heckle them (don't confuse this for positive behaviours, which can be similar!).

Watch also how the band reacts to the crowd. Battles of the Bands have "audience participation" as a criterion for a reason. Watching the crowd can give you a very strong sense of a band's performance.

Crowd reactions can be vital, especially if you find yourself at a show that you don't like. It's happened to me that I had to cover a show (there's been more than one) of a genre I intensely dislike, of bands I'd prefer to burn than see live, and even of bands that I have never heard before. Watching the crowd gave me far more material than just the music, and enabled me to write a fair review: focusing on the band and how the band played. In some cases, I managed to get happy commentary from fans, which is high praise indeed.

It's important to remember that the crowd reaction can balance out your own personal preferences, when you're a music critic. You can't routinely shit on a band in your reviews simply because you don't like what they play. Preferably you won't cover these shows; but when you have to, the crowd is an essential levelling tool.

6. Properties of the venue

While you're watching the band/crowd reaction (and hopefully enjoying the set too!) try to move around inside the room to get a sense of the sound and the mix. It's good to be able to report this kind of thing. Your readers will get a greater sense of environment if you can tell them that closer to the stage the sound was muddy, yet near the doors you could hear everything beautifully.

There are some venues in which the sound is only good at the mixing desk. There are some where the sound is not affected by movement; some can't take low-end at all; some you can't hear the percussion; some are plagued by problems (broken or ineffective mics, blown-out or crap speakers, etc.); some are great until whoever's behind the desk decides to 'fix' things—usually resulting in making things worse.

Also, if it's a huge show (like Carcass, for example), take note of the lighting, any video that may be running, any special effects, and so on. Take note of whether these elements added to, or detracted from, the performance. Some bands like to rely more on their special effects than on their stage work, for example; and it's not always a good outcome.

Each and every element will add another layer of texture to your review of the show.

7. Remember why everything is important

While all of these elements are properly outside the review of the bands, they all contribute to the way in which the show runs, and to punter satisfaction. As a music journo that heads out to review gigs, you are not just someone absorbing the performance of the band. That is a big part of it, of course, but there is so much more going on than just the bands playing.

A metal gig is a gathering of a community—so covering a show is way more than just watching a band play. There are bigger interactions at stake, not least the fact that a band's performance can be correlated with an audience's response.

It's a two-way street. And it's not one that a stranger to the community can easily make sense of. This is why a good ethnographic foundation is important: you are not only going into a community to observe its goings-on; you are part of that community.

START PRACTICING

Given that there is so much in this chapter, try to get out to a few shows, some you like, some you don't, and take notice of what's going on around you, on all levels. Make notes if you feel the need (sometimes it's essential), and when you get home try to sit down straight away and write it all up creatively.

Try to recreate the experience from what you noticed at the show. Work into your piece some of your preliminary material, too. Tell your reader a good story. If there are no specific adventures, try to weave it well enough that whoever reads it could be drawn into the experience of the show.

When you've done that, put it away for a few days, and don't think about it. When those few days have passed, pull it out and read through it, with fresh eyes.

What sort of reaction do you have to it? What would you do differently? And more importantly, how do you think, now you've had the distance of time, that a fresh reader would react?

3. WHAT'S THIS 'CRITIQUE'?

Critique. *noun*. A detailed analysis and assessment of something, esp. a literary, philosophical, or political theory.[16]

When I was an undergraduate at university, I was lucky enough to study criticism, under one of Australia's very best theatre critics, Myk Mykyta[11]. By 'theatre', I'm sure you understand me to mean 'of the stage' as opposed to 'of the screen', although I did study film criticism with Myk as well.

I was one of those students who loved what I did so much that I paid very close attention to what I was learning. I also put it into practise by writing film and book critique for the university's student paper, *Entropy*. During this time I was very prolific: I wrote fiction, essays, poetry, and criticism for *Entropy*. And in the last half of my uni time (I was also one of those students who were at uni for a long time) I was a key music critic and writer as well.

This time spent putting my studies into personal practise taught me some very valuable things. One of the key learnings I took from it is that critique is exactly the same across all art forms; all that differs is in the execution and in its finer points. My further reading—not of theory, but simply of master critics, in all fields—has reinforced this notion over and over again.

The defining elements of criticism, the theory, philosophy, and ideas behind it, are the same no matter what type of critique you're writing.

This is why, when I had the honour of sitting on a panel about critique at Format Festival one year, next to my tutor and mentor Myk Mykyta, he agreed with every major point that I raised, and (much to my inner suck-up student) astounded me by reinforcing and talking back to them. He was the only theatre critic present, I was the only music critic present; all the rest were book critics. The output and the form studied might be different, but we were all speaking the same language. It was enormously good fun, and such good brain food.

Unfortunately, what one tends to find now is that a vast number of active critics, especially online, are young and unschooled. In worst-case scenarios, they are also unedited.

I have blogged about this an awful lot in past years, but it is true: the majority of those critiquing and curating our musical culture now (largely) lack critical training. They're often uni grads or students, which one hopes gives them some semblance of critical thinking ability, but they are not critics by learning. What they learn, they pick up on the job.

Which is very interesting. Allow me to digress in order to contextualise. When I studied editing, for example, it was a new thing for universities to offer; it had previously been a trade, something you learn on the job with someone else as your mentor. The old-school constantly moaned about the fact that it was no longer a trade.

Back in the day, journalists tended to 'fall into' criticism jobs, and they too learned on the job. My favourite critic, Clive James[12], started at uni, writing for *Honi Soit*, and his work gradually became noticed by greater and greater publications.

While there are more and more courses for 'music' or 'rock journalists', and greater interest in music journalism as a whole (there was even a workshop in it at the Byron Bay Writers' Festival in 2011, for fuck's sake), proffered studies in criticism itself have not increased. A quick search of university courses in Australia will tell you that there are very few that focus on criticism. The ones that do are primarily textual criticism courses; and as much as I love textual critique, many of these courses simply provide a grounding in literary theory. It's vastly different ground. Literary or textual critique is interesting, but it's not the type of critique we're talking about here.

And, on the other hand, offering defined streams of journalism in music is stupid: it is irrelevant, and it makes kids think there are jobs in the field. Which there aren't, unless you're happy being paid in promotional MP3s;

although, most property managers will not accept your rent in Axel Rudi Pell promo CDs.

The point I was trying to make is that, to a large extent, the critics you have now, and will have in the future, are not trained by books or theory. They learn by example, and, only if they're lucky, learn via interaction with a good editor or mentor. Otherwise it's much like I learned the niceties: trial and error.

Most young people don't have the benefit of what I did, which was a solid grounding in the required elements of criticism theory and philosophy. Which brings us back to the 'learning on the job' method mentioned earlier.

But the real question, the million-dollar, money-shot question, is, do music critics need it? If I, as someone who learned through a combination of 'books' and 'trade' came out alright, and the critics of old learned via 'trade' exclusively, what point do I have even comparing the two?

It's a valid question. And it is, I think, a necessary one.

While I like to think that critics do well to learn the foundations of writing and editing, the greater part of me believes that the trade learning—for switched-on people—is more important. If one is unable to draw learnings from multiple places, and has no great desire for constant learning, one is better off learning to paint houses.

I don't say this idly. Allow me to quote Clive James, who in turn quoted great Italian critic, Eugenio Montale[13]:

"Mastery is knowing how to limit yourself".

Furthermore, Clive James worked according to

> "... his belief that a cultural commentator could only
> benefit from being as involved as possible with his subject,
> and over as wide a range as opportunity allowed."

Which means that you can learn from books, but you absolutely must be making, and taking, the time to put what you are learning into practise. As much as possible. In every way possible.

If you're a music critic, this means being involved in news writing and presentation, in interviews, in release reviews, in gig reviews, in thinking of articles to write that you may need to research yourself, that are outside of the standard 'interview feature' interface.

But you also need to know how to reign in your verbosity, and to find your niche. No amount of education will teach you how to limit yourself.

What one learns, if one has an undying interest in the field of criticism, is that the masters are masters for a reason. And you can only learn that by knowing who they are. This is where universities come in so handy: they give you lists of references, force you to read writers you would never have read before. And if you are working in the trade at the same time—as one would hope—their ways and wiles will cement themselves more closely in your brain. Most likely because you have greater opportunity for imitation.

Imitation, let's never forget, is one of the best ways of learning a writing style.

In some study notes that I read about Eugenio Montale[14], it was pointed out in really rather bland terms about why Montale was such a great critic. Allow me to share:

> "...his overriding concern as a critic is with the essential qualities and effects of achieved art, and not with the problems—a stable occupation of a professional critic—relating to its genesis, source, and influence, or problems relating to its historical, philosophical, and philological aspects ... With a sharp and unerring eye on what is significant and relevant in a work of art, Montale talks about it in a straightforward and unpretentious manner, without wasting his time or energy in composing elaborately rhetorical periods."

And in turn, Montale wrote about Matthew Arnold[15], that Arnold's criticism

> "...comes from an intelligence that, even if not trained to some kinds of rigour, had its own discipline; an intelligence that is informed by a mature and delicate sense of the humane values and can manifest itself directly as a fine sensibility."

What you find, when you start reading through the works and lives of the great critics, is that each of them is defined by a 'fine sensibility'. Moreso than through their training 'to some kinds of rigour'.

I would argue that each of the critics mentioned here—which also includes the excellent Myk Mykyta—could have their work defined by that 'fine sensibility'.

It is the works, the intelligence, the deployment of art that makes critics great, not necessarily the formal training that they undertake. It is the ways in which they limit their prose, do not overstate things, and only look at what is relevant to the work of art and to the art form, that makes them great.

Excellent critics do not write for a consumer group, necessarily. The point of critique is not *should I should I not buy* XYZ. The point is *critique*: an analysis and assessment of a work of art on its own merits.

This is perhaps the most important point of this chapter. What is critique? A detailed analysis and assessment of elements that are relevant to a work of art, and to the art form, that makes them great.

The second-most important point? That the analysis and assessment is focused on a work of art on its own merits. That is, without relation to the creator's history, discography, or place in an overall genre. An evaluation independent of the influence of any creation to either side.

If we were to turn the generic definition of critique around slightly, and apply it to music journalism, we would come to a slightly different statement. This statement must needs include reference to the type of art that it is (music), and also, preferably, to the subgenre of music—and so on down until you define it clearly.

With regards to metal, this becomes important: each of metal's subgenres have specifics and requirements that may or may not apply to any other subgenre, and which are unlikely to apply to any other genre of music. Other elements, such as performance and musicianship, are fairly universal.

We would also re-visit the final statement, 'that makes them great', because we are generally not talking about classic works. We are talking about any works. Therefore, the elements to which we refer are relevant to a work of art, and to the art form, that makes those elements what they are.

This notion of 'what they are' is important in musical critique. You want to assess a recording, or a performance, as per how it appears. Don't strain your brain, think like a Taoist. Things are what they are. You need to evaluate musical art on its own terms, first. It is only when you have a solid grasp of that, that you can start to speculate.

On its own merits, first. Only later can you think about historical or environmental placement thought and philosophy.

We could re-cast the definition of music critique, for an album, thusly:

> A detailed analysis and assessment of all elements relevant to a recording (mix and overall sound, artwork, lyrics, song-writing ability, musicianship, length) and to the genre (and subgenre, which might include genre fit, success of experimentation, and so on) that makes them what they are.

And for a performance:

> A detailed analysis and assessment of all elements relevant to a musical performance (mix and overall sound, lighting, musicianship, enthusiasm and energy, stage craft, audience interaction, vibe and venue, length of set, style of set, songs included in the set) and to the genre (and subgenre, which might include genre fit, success of experimentation in a live setting, contribution to the overall "text" of live performances in metal, and so on) that makes it what it is.

Once you have a bit of a grasp on evaluating things in their own states can you begin to speculate. Great critics can place a band, or a band's artwork, in a greater context; they can write stories around them, place them in a historical setting, and generally work some magic with the hows and wherefores of a critical assessment.

It is at this point that you can consider thinking about an album's contribution to the genre as a whole, contribution to the band's discography; or a performance's contribution to the overall "text" of live performances in the genre.

Lasting criticism has the ability to weave both the 'as it is' portion with the 'what gives it is place' portion, seamlessly.

And it is at least halfway to this point that this book will drive you. The rest of the journey is yours to make through reflection, learning, and hard work.

4. REVIEWING A BAND'S PERFORMANCE

By now you will have a basic understanding of ethnography, criticism, and the foundational principles of both. You will also—hopefully—have put your principles into practice in all sorts of locations, from your mate's house to shows, thereby sharpening your writing ability. You will be gaining a finer understanding of how to try and recreate the atmosphere of a show for those destined to be your readers.

All of the above is essential, but as a music journalist you will not get very far if you do not have a basic understanding of how to review a band's performance.

Remember: if you are not a writer first and a fan second, and that if you do not practice your skills, then this book—no matter how badly you might want to work in the field—is going to be relatively pointless for you. A good music journalist is not a groupie or fan boy: it is a person for whom recreating and evaluating performances in writing is at the top of the tree.

Journalists need professional distance

It is well to remember that you are in the role of critic as a music journalist. The word 'critic', a dodgy article about 'critics' at Wikipedia[10] tells us, comes from the Greek 'kritikos', meaning 'able to discern'. Furthermore, the article states:

"…which is a Greek derivation of the word κριτής (krités), meaning a person who offers reasoned judgment or analysis, value judgment, interpretation, or observation[2]. The term can be used to describe an adherent of a position disagreeing with or opposing the object of criticism.

"Modern critics include professionals or amateurs who regularly judge or interpret performances or other works (such as those of artists, scientists, musicians, or actors), and typically publish their observations, often in periodicals. Critics are numerous in certain fields, including art, music, film, theatre or drama, restaurant, and scientific publication critics."

All of this tells you that you need to approach your evaluation of a band's performance with a certain professional distance. You have to analyse, judge, interpret a performance through a range of criteria. As the previous chapter briefly outlined, you need to analyse and assess an album or performance on its own merits.

However, there are certain criteria that are essential in analysing and assessing performances of bands. These criteria I will get to presently.

What you come up against when you review metal bands, particularly, are the Metal Geeks: fans who know everything about everything, or at least like to think they do. If you are not a Metal Geek yourself, you need not worry if you are honest in your review and can evaluate a performance fairly dispassionately. The best metal journos are indeed metal geeks; but like anything in life, if you stick with what you do, you will pick up enough knowledge to begin to qualify as a minor rank Geek yourself.

I've written metal journalism for years and I'm not even halfway to being as much of a Geek as those around me. I do, however, write, study, and research. I am also honest; so if I don't know something, I don't pretend to know it. I'd rather admit my ignorance than be called out on it and be unable to defend myself.

Music criticism versus other types of criticism

Realistically, evaluating the performance of a band is not starkly different to evaluating or reviewing any other type of performance art: film, theatre, street performance or performance art. There are different types of things you have to take into consideration, true; but the essence of the work is very similar across the board.

In theatre, dance, or performance criticism you would need to consider what the scene or dance looks like, who wrote the play (or choreographed the dance) and a bit of its history, how the mood was set and to what effect, who each of the major players are and what their individual performances were like—and how they related to the whole—and so on.

In film, too, you need to evaluate the story, how it presented on screen, what the sound, lighting, cast were like, who various people were in the crew and what role the played; and you need to relate it all to the whole piece.

I believe that, in criticism, the adage 'more than the sum of its parts' is very apt. You can analyse, interpret, judge, and critique each part of a performance; but if you do not relate those parts to the whole then you are going to lose a certain element of what you set out to achieve in the beginning.

Performance: What to look for

The elements of performance that you need to take into consideration are as follows:

1. The energy and performance of each individual band member.

Did their energy stay at its peak for the entire set? How did he/she perform? What his/her performance unmarred by errors—e.g. were sweep arpeggios even and nicely placed, or double-kicks well executed? If there were errors, how did the band member deal with that? Take it in his/her stride or get progressively, and noticeably, annoyed? What does observing this band member tell you about band dynamics as a whole?

2. The energy and performance of the band as a unit.

When you piece together the individual members' performances in your mind, does your evaluation of the band as a whole follow along naturally? If it doesn't, then there is something amiss that you need to look for because it is hurting the band's performance—and you need to be able to explain what that something is. What are the band dynamics like? Do they 'play well" together? What is the collective vibe like, and what does it tell you about the band?

3. How the band members (individually and as a band) interact with the audience.

This is always a criterion that is way up there, as I mentioned early in this book, in judging check-lists for battles of the bands and competitions, and as a youngster I could never understand why. Having gotten into this field, I now do.

Let me explain it for you. It is because of the fact that when a band can effortlessly interact with a crowd—get them to chant, to cheer, to stick their horns in the air—and when a band is effortlessly relating to a crowd to the point where the individual audience members have almost forgotten everyone else in the venue—that is when you know that the band has something special. Highly experienced bands often don't even have to try, but younger bands do, and done badly it is very, very painful to watch. Some bands play entire sets with their backs to the audience. Needless to say, if a band does not interact at all, then the audience (and the critic) loses interest incredibly quickly.

4. What the band sounds like.

Can you hear the guitars? The bass? The drums? The vocalist(s)? The keyboards (if any)? Is there a good balance? If not, is it the venue's fault, the sound engineer's fault, or the band's fault? And if you do pick one to blame, can you back up your claim with solid reasoning (such as, this venue always sounds like crap regardless of the sound guy, and it is both common knowledge and often a subject of discussion)? Feel free to relate this type of analysis to your analysis of the venue's sound and what the environment is like: they are interrelated, after all.

5. What the band looks like.

Yes, we all know it is not a beauty pageant. But have you ever paid good money to see a band you've always wanted to see, and the band did everything right, but they all looked like they'd rather be at home playing their PS3s? It totally ruins the atmosphere and your own (and others') enjoyment of the show.

Some bands can look like shit, because they're near the end of a tour for example, but manage to overcome that while on stage. You need to be able to give your readers a bit of a sense of what it was like being in the audience, so what the band looked like can be important. It can also be particularly important if you're reviewing specific genres. If any costuming (e.g. corpse paint or spikes) looks farcical, feminine, or just plain stupid, it's your job to say so, and to point out why.

6. Evaluate the set list.

If you are critiquing the performance of a major band (in the same league as, say Napalm Death, Cannibal Corpse, Destruction, etc.)—and even if you're not, but it's of more importance if you are—then you need to evaluate the set list. What did they play? Did they play it well? How long was the set? Were there any encores (why not, if not)? What songs were played as encores?

Remember that if you are seeing a band on their first visit to somewhere, then you are going to want to hear a great spread from a band's discography. If it's a tour to promote a particular album, then you are going to want to hear that album. This is where some research ahead of time, or good Geeky knowledge, will stand you in good stead for the writing of your review. Also, remember to watch for the crowds' reaction to the set list, because if you are not a fan yourself then you will miss important indicators if you don't stay alert.

7. Other things to look for: responses to hecklers, general mood, etc.

When you're reviewing a band that has a great sense of humour, they will tell good (or crap) jokes; they will respond to hecklers in the crowd, especially if the hecklers mean well (as they often do); they will look like they're enjoying themselves; and the vibe will generally be a warm one. If you encounter a humourless or moody band, they won't respond to hecklers; they will not engage in much 'conversation', let alone jokes; and the vibe will be different again. Each of these is important. Keep a running commentary, if you're quick enough, of what the band members say to the audience, what jokes they tell, and so on: it all helps you recreate the atmosphere and provide a good sense of the show afterwards. Trust me, you won't remember it accurately if you don't write these things down!

Tying all of the elements together

Once you are back at your desk and writing up your review, including each of these elements should come naturally to you: especially if you have taken good notes and have a good sense of what to look out for before you go to the show. If you are a writer first and a fan second, then it will be even easier for you.

If neither of these things describe you, then you need to write out the performance from beginning to end. What was your first impression of the band when they came out on stage? What was your very first impression of what they sounded like, how they related to each other and to the audience? Did they play as well/fast/heavy as you thought (or hoped) that they would?

The best advice I can give you at this point, though, is to trust your gut instinct and be honest. Write your own opinion into the review, support every single statement with good reasoning, so your readers know exactly why you are making that statement. And make sure that nothing you write is generic.

More details about how to write up your piece will come later, and specific guidelines come up in *PRO TIP 1—Get the Words Right*.

5. REVIEWING A NEW RELEASE

Reviewing a band's performance, and getting your ethnography skills down pat, is just one aspect of a music journalist's job. By far the most time-consuming of all tasks is reviewing releases. Music journos are frequently referred to as "reviewers". I hate this terminology with a passion, because for me, a 'reviewer' and a 'critic' are two very different things. I went on about this at some length earlier, but if you are serious about your work, you will be equally serious about the differences between reviewers and critics.

This chapter looks at the skills, abilities, and knowledge that you need to critique a release, and do it well. The next chapter will help you out with your ability to write an insightful review. The two skills are very different, and are each worthy of separate examination and discussion.

So, what do you need to critique a release well? You require: an ability to listen to an album for what it is a knowledge of bands, genres, and discographies a critical ear a distanced and dispassionate perspective. From this list, you might think that being a critic is about being disengaged. Not at all! Rather, it demonstrates that fans are not necessarily in the best position to review an album. Very few drooling fans can listen to any release with a distanced and dispassionate perspective. For proof, all you need to do is go and read a few threads of the Iron Maiden forums.

Listen to an album for what it is

If you get into this line of work—even as a volunteer—then if you're any good at what you do then you find yourself drowning in releases within a short period of time. On the one hand it's great because your skill is acknowledged (and you get a lot of new music regularly); on the other hand, you can find yourself not knowing which way to turn, or not knowing how to proceed with each subsequent review. Now, when you start to feel like this, spare a thought for your editor, who is experiencing this on a far larger scale. (Editors, you can hit Chapter 14 for tips on managing your workload.)

One of the first things of which you quickly become aware as a release reviewer, is that you need to develop—very quickly—the ability to listen to a release for what it is. It is very easy—and a deep trap—to find yourself comparing an album to the last one you heard. This applies not just to the last album that you heard by the same band, but also to the immediate past release you've had on your stereo, in your iTunes, on your iPod, or on a label's promo streamer site. This can cause immense problems when you have, say, metalcore, death core, death/groove, thrash, and NWOBHM releases to get through all in one day. It is even more of a problem if you're a huge fan of one genre, and don't particularly like one or more of the others.

Being able to listen to a release for what it is, isn't something that can necessarily be taught. It comes, instead, from the experience of being put in the position where you suddenly realise that your writing is being generated in the context of a swathe of other 'material'. The learning part of it is becoming aware of the fact that this situation is muddying your output.

However, there are some key things you can do that can help. some of these include: having a break between releases. Listening to albums one on top of the other is a sure-fire method of getting them mixed up in your mind mixing up genres wherever possible. If you listen to five death metal albums in a row, for instance, pretty soon they each start to take on the flavour of the others you've heard. Listening critically first. This is expanded upon below; for now, you need to be aware that if you listen critically first, you are in a better position to pick up an album's unique nuances sooner researching an album as extensively as possible either while listening, or soon after (before you listen to any others) practicing differentiating between albums of similar style or genre whenever possible. You may find that you begin to develop other methods of differentiation unique to yourself. No method is incorrect; the important thing is disallowing one album to influence your take of another.

Build your knowledge of a genre, a band, and a band's discography

There are music nerds—and, in particular, metal nerds—absolutely everywhere. I am not one of them. It helps enormously if you are one of those people who easily retains knowledge of genres, studios, and bands.

If you're not a music geek, the quickest way of being taken for a sham is to expose your lack of knowledge of a genre, a band, or a band's discography through writing careless commentary. While the absolute best way of addressing a gap in your knowledge is to listen deeply and broadly across a genre and across a band's discography, there are some ways in which you can address it in the interim.

One of these is to read the one-sheet provided with a promotional album. These are excellent; but I direct your attention to Pro Tip 1: Be careful of the one-sheet for an explanation about why relying on one-sheets is dangerous territory. Never forget that one-sheets are written by publicists with the aim of selling the album: to stores, to journalists, to the industry. One-sheets look like informative documents (and very often are this), but they are primarily selling tools. It behoves you to remember this.

Hitting up various websites for specific information is probably one of the best ways of gaining information, and getting it quickly. A word of warning, however: if you don't know what you're looking for, then you are not going to find quality information. Easily the quickest way of gaining the information you are after—whether for this purpose or any other—is to work out exactly what you want and need to know. It is no good going through Encyclopaedia Metallum (for instance) to find band information if you are not clear on what you want to know. For the purposes of finding label information, genre information, or notes about a release, then you have to know where and how to look for it.

Occasionally, reading other critics' reviews of the same album can help. A word of warning, however: doing this is likely to muddy your own perceptions of a release, especially if you have not engaged in critical listening of an album first, and made your own notes for a start. If you do have a strong sense of your own reaction, it is fine to see how others perceived it, and how they wrote about the release. If you don't, then you'll quickly find yourself regurgitating what some other critic wrote, without clearly understanding how or why a review was written in a particular way.

A knowledge of genre stands you in good stead for evaluating how a band works within that genre; it also helps you to analyse how a band might be warping a genre, creating crossovers, or generating a new post-genre style. The other reason for increasing your knowledge of a genre is that it gives you the ability to write knowledgeably about the context for the release, and the ability to compare that release to others of a similar style. And, of course, it helps you to identify the best audience for an album.

A knowledge of a band similarly stands you in good stead for how a band has evolved to its latest point. It might have gained or lost members, changed its preferred engineers or studios, changed labels, or changed its approach to the music. Knowing all of this gives you the background knowledge to be able to write about a release with clarity and insightfulness: two things that are going to make your work stand apart from anybody else's.

Similarly, knowing a band's discography—and being familiar with it—can help you achieve the same thing. Take a band like Samael for example: they began in black metal, evolved through to become a largely industrial/black/electro band, and then started to pick up on their roots again. The extent of that band's evolution is only evident once you have heard nearly everything they've produced. If you have no way of hearing a band's entire discography (which is likely for most people, except those who have been in the business a long time—or who are huge fans), then the internet can help you. Watch film clips on YouTube, hit up bands' websites, or MySpace or Reverbnation, or Facebook pages, and try to get a sense or feel for a band any way you can. Sometimes, if you don't mind admitting your ignorance, talking to people who are fans of the band can help enormously.

Develop a critical ear

Working your way up to being able to listen to a release critically is similar to being critical about a band's performance. This is far harder if you are a fan of a band than it is if you are coming across a release or band for the first time, or if you do not have any emotional ties to a band or its output.

Possessing a good critical ear means being able to assess several things: performance, production values, the sense of the 'band' coming through in a release, the band's take on a genre and its performance within it, the flow of an album, the quality of the song writing, and so on.

It is important to listen critically first, and for pleasure afterwards. If you enjoy an album just for the sake of it, that's great. But it hampers your ability to write critically because you never got a handle on the critical elements right from the beginning. Here's a bit of a run-down of what you need to be able to assess.

In listening to a release, you must be able to assess the top- and bottom-end of the sound. Often, especially in metal releases, the bottom end can be muddy (hard to hear or muffled), or you get a real 'high-end irritation' caused by the treble being just too high hear where elements are placed in the mix. If the vocals are really loud and dominate the music, then chances are that the vocals are too high in the mix; similarly, if you can't really hear the bass line, it's too far down or mixed out so far that the bass may as well not be there. If there are other elements (atmospheric keyboards, violins, accordions, fiddles, female vocals, samples, electronic elements, synths, etc) then you are likely to be able to get a real feeling for whereabouts in the mix these are placed. It helps to try to 'visualise' the music while you listen: you are often able to picture each element in the mix as being on a different layer assess the production values. Production values differ to the mix, though frequently the two become confused in writers' minds. Is the album too clear, too polished-sounding, or is it crusty as hell? You can usually tell. Demos, for instance, often sound like they're recorded in someone's back shed, while releases by professional bands can be so highly 'produced' that they come out sounding almost digital. I wrote many years about an album sounding like it was recorded in a back shed; and the band wrote to me to tell me that that was exactly what happened. So, to their minds, the production values were a perfect representation of what they had wanted to achieve. Establish what are—to you—the worst elements, and be able to explain what they are and why they are the worst establish what are—to you—the best elements, and be able to explain what they are and why they are the best explain the experience of the entire album. It's great if you can talk about the progression of the album, the placement of the tracks within it, and get a sense for whether the track-listing is perhaps in the best order for this release explain your experience of particular tracks get a handle on the lyrics or the theme for a release. This isn't always possible, but for some bands it can be absolutely critical that you do.

Remember that no release is ever perfect. It is incredibly rare that you get 100% perfect, and equally odd to get one that is total trash. There are always poor, and redeeming, elements of nearly every album that you hear. The difficult part is recognising them and being able to talk about them with clarity and good reasoning.

In some respects you could argue that doing all of the above will turn you into a fence-sitter. Get used to it and find a comfortable fence, because if you review a lot of albums, sitting on a fence is where you will end up.

The importance of a distanced and dispassionate perspective

Throughout this book I've been talking very strongly about the necessity of being able to maintain your credibility, and of being a writer first and a fan second. The first comes from the latter; and the latter is most important when you are reviewing albums.

A distanced and dispassionate perspective does two things: it divorces you from your emotional attachment to a release, and it enables you to see clearly.

The Wikipedia entry on Criticism places a great deal of emphasis on 'democratic judgement':

> "Criticism is the activity of judgement or informed interpretation and, in many cases, can be synonymous with 'analysis'."(17)

Similarly, the comments on the Film Criticism page(18) are equally pertinent:

> "... Film critics working for newspapers, magazines, broadcast media, and online publications, mainly review new releases. Normally they only see any given film once and have only a day or two to formulate opinions.[citation needed] Despite this, critics have an important impact on films, especially those of certain genres. The popularity of mass-marketed action, horror, and comedy films tend not to be greatly affected by a critic's overall judgment of a film. The plot summary and description of a film that makes up the majority of any film review can have an important impact on whether people decide to see a film. For prestige films with a limited release, such as independent dramas, the influence of reviews is extremely important. Poor reviews will often doom a film to obscurity and financial loss.

> "...

> "Since so much money is riding on positive reviews, studios often work to woo film critics. Any major release is accompanied by mailings to film critics press kits containing background information, many photos for use in a publication, and often small gifts. Film reviewers who appear on television are given clips from the movie which they may use."

I do know for a fact that some major labels like to bribe journalists to recast negative reviews of their artists, or to ensure positive reviews, and that a lot of work goes into prepping journalists in order to give the label or distro the best possible chances of a good review. I also know well that there is a huge debate about the interface between promo and marketing: whether good promotion (and good reviews) actually helps to sell more releases; and I know too that a good journalist will gain the respect of labels and distros in his or her field.

Whether you work in film, book, or music criticism is of little matter, because the skills are largely the same. You just need to learn to pick up different elements of the art form with which you are engaged.

But despite all of this, the fact is that unless you have a distanced and dispassionate perspective, you are not going to write honest criticism. You do only have a short timeframe in which to listen to, and write about, a release; and you do have to be honest about your work. If you are a fan boy or groupie, for example, and you are writing reviews of bands you like (and doing so exclusively), then chances are that you will have a low credibility rating. Chances are, too, that your output is likely to be poor, because you are unable to gain enough 'distance' in order to see the release as it is. It is vital to get a critical sense of an album, and of a band's performance, and you can't do that if you are too close to it. 8. Reviewing a new release: stage two The previous chapter of this course will hopefully have made you excited about learning the nitty-gritties of writing your release review, after having honed your critical ear. This chapter will show you some of the traps to watch out for—including why imitation can be flattering to others, but why it's not necessarily a good thing. It will also take you through form and structure, key elements that must be included, and how to turn your critical notes into insightful commentary.

As mentioned several times earlier in the book, the art of criticism is applicable across nearly any art form. Your style will change according to what you are reviewing, as will some key elements, but the basics and tenets of good, effective criticism are almost infinitely flexible.

Find your point and stick to it (or, succinct writing is essential)

In writing for any publication, in print or otherwise, it is rare that you are given the luxury of being verbose. Most publications allow a maximum of 500 words per review; meaning, therefore, that everything has to be squished into a couple of paragraphs. By 'everything', I am of course referring to all of your critical notes, including your assessment of an album's production (top- and bottom-end, production values, and where elements are placed in the mix), the best elements, the worst elements, your experience of particular tracks, lyrical themes, artwork, and so on.

Writing succinctly is an art in and of itself. One of the world's masters of criticism, expat-Australian Clive James, tied the notion up very neatly in a review of Robert Hughes's *The Fatal Shore* (1988) when he stated that good journalism is: '… seeing the point and keeping to it'.(19)

In my experience, the easiest way of sticking to your point is seeing what that point is in the first place. It gives you a notional framework within which everything else you write fits, and helps you to structure your review in such a way that you are able to prove that your point is valid.

To define what your point is, ask yourself what you think of the album. Don't refer to your notes, just recall the experience of it and think of three or four words that sum it up. You might find that a release demonstrates a band's evolution in a particular direction, or a growing maturity in a genre. You might find that it made you want to saw your leg off with a blunt saw rather than listen to it a second time, or perhaps even to listen to the second half. Whatever it is, this is the whole point of your review: you must somehow pull your notes together to support this contention.

Understand what is required of you

Now that you know what you are going to write about, you must get a handle on what the publication requires of you. Almost every publication of any quality has a dedicated style guide that ensures every article within it has a certain titular style, a certain formatting style, and—if it's online—that certain keyword fields are completed.

If you are provided with a style guide and you don't use it, you will irritate your editor very quickly. You will also find yourself shuffled down the list of priority writers, and that you miss out on important or key releases more and more often. Those who follow instructions easily, will naturally be less work for those who edit and/or moderate it. Take heed: this might not seem important, but it is vital if you seek longevity in the industry.

Once you've got a handle on the necessary styles, which will guide the physical elements of what you write, and you know roughly the shape into which you must mold your review, it's time to put pen to paper. Or, rather, fingers to the keys.

Form and structure are important

Writing a release review is not rocket science: fan boys do it, groupies do it, bored people do it for something to do, and most music journalists (and metal journos in particular) are not writers in the first instance. If you are a writer in the first instance, then you will have a far more mature style and a greater grasp on both language and the micro elements of writing (like punctuation). You will also be less likely to simply imitate somebody else's style—more on that later.

Put simply, a good review will: provide a summary at the start that gives a basic overview, demonstrating the point to which you are going to stick discuss the overall experience of the album, weaving in the production values, any startling or interesting facts about it (such as guest appearances, or its origins or history), giving the reader a sense of the album as a whole highlight stand-out tracks, or tracks on an album that demonstrate your point, or which are worthy of mentioning due to stylistic variation, particular skills that the band display, demonstration of changes in style from one album to another, or other interesting or striking elements. These will come out of your critical notes: for example, you might review a black metal album with a remixed electronic version as a bonus track, and that would be worth mentioning; similarly, a great old-school thrash album that features one track full of breakdowns and metalcore vocal styles would be odd for other reasons, and is similarly worthy of particular attention sum up the album in a final paragraph, with an assessment of it in terms of listener experience, band history, genre, and any other points that you may have missed; you may also include here a recommendation to the reader as to whether or not it is something on which he or she is recommended hard-earned money on include a final line with label and release date, or purchase details, if it is required by your publication. Appreciate your own style

Some publications out there—like *Terrorizer*, *Metal Hammer* and others—have writers who display styles that are instantly recognisable. Some reviewers have a style that I personally don't like: reviews filled with analogies, and strings of adjectives and other descriptors that obfuscate the review. Reading one or two is good fun; reading more than that gets old very quickly. Clarity and simplicity are far more effective in the long-run.

Whether or not I do or do not like a particular style is of no regard to this text, or to your learning. But, an absolute sin is trying to imitate a style like that without really understanding how to do it. Imitation may be the sincerest form of flattery—except for writers. Writers who shamelessly imitate another style lay themselves open to ridicule, especially if that style is identifiable. It can also slow the development of your own style, much to your detriment.

Far better is to go with who you are and what you do: have a 'take no prisoners' and 'fuck 'em all' attitude. Eventually—that is, if you don't start out your journalistic life with a writing style you'd be happy to call your own—you will develop one. That style is defined by certain phrases that you favour, the types of analogies you use, your own peculiar sense of humour (or lack thereof), your level of pedantry, how informed you are, how you wield your punctuation, and much more besides. Your 'voice', much like your fingerprint, is unique.

Writing is an art form that people take seriously, because it morphs the language you use every day into a more formal style. Therefore, while you may not be confident about your style initially, you can at least appreciate that you have the balls to put pen to paper in your own way; confidence follows with practise.

Common pitfalls

Writing a review seems easy, doesn't it? That's because, if we're going to be honest with our readers, it is. However, there are several pitfalls it is worth being aware of, in order to avoid them.

Here is a list of things to avoid.

1. Filling your review with strings of adjectives and analogies.

A writer who goes the long way about describing something does not have a clear idea of what he or she wanted to say in the first place. It is far better to be clear: one simple, effective analogy will beat a line of convoluted descriptors or vague analogies any day.

2. Being too geeky and filling your review with information that is irrelevant to the release under scrutiny.

It can sometimes be a fine line between being helpful and being overly geeky, especially with a band that has been around for a long time. It is tempting to display one's knowledge about a discography, or how changes in band members have affected the sound of a band. I have four words for you: it is not necessary. Save that sort of thing for interview write-ups, where the information is actually valuable.

3. Describing every single track in detail.

Unless there is a very good reason (such as a concept album for which you cannot get a full sense without talking about how the tracks fit together to complete the concept), it is boring to read.

4. Talking about one track as though it is indicative of the entire album, without saying whether it is or not.

Your reader will start to wonder whether you only listened to one track in order to get out of your review cheaply.

5. Writing statements of which you are not one hundred per cent certain.

If you are even slightly in doubt about something, make sure you check it —whether it's the name of an engineer, the sound of a particular song that you can't quite recall, or whereabouts the album was recorded. Similarly, if you are stating that an album is a milestone (like, the tenth or fifteenth full-length), make sure you're right. Nothing destroys your credibility quicker than basic inaccuracies.

6. Omitting an assessment of the production values of an album.

It might be a fabulous cock-rock release, but if the production values are like early Beherit, and you don't mention it (and if people go out and buy the release on your recommendation) then you'll find yourself creating more enemies than fans. If you haven't heard Beherit, take the time to go and hear it so you know what I mean. Words can't do it justice. (It's very noisy.)

7. Failing to proofread or spell-check your review.

The basics of good writing are essential. Make sure you proofread what you write—better yet, read it aloud to see if really does make sense—and check your spelling. Do that and the people in the office will really appreciate your work.

Checking your review... and letting it sit for a day

Before you finish and submit your review, it's a good idea to check your review against your notes, and to run it past someone that you trust, for feedback purposes. Ask yourself whether you can gain a clear sense of the release, and the listening experience of the release, from what you've written. Are any key points left out? Would you consider your review to be insightful? Have you made too much of some elements and not enough of others?

It's always a good idea to let your writing sit for a day or so before you go back to it for this purpose. It helps to give you some distance from your work, so you read it more objectively. Never be afraid of completely rewriting your work, especially if it doesn't sit right. A good self-edit can often make the difference between a good review and an outstanding one: changing a word here and there will not have the same power as completely recasting a paragraph.

Reading your work to someone else—especially if that someone else has heard the release—can also be very beneficial. That person may suggest something you've left out, or may query a phrase that they don't understand. While a critical review is always mere opinion, a second perspective can be invaluable.

6. INTERVIEWS

Preparation & Running the Show

It is no secret that interviewing bands is a nerve-wracking affair. Most interviews you read are conducted by highly experienced music journalists, and it seems that they set the bar pretty high. Fear not—even if you need to meet an extraordinarily high standard, there is a method that can set you going in the right direction.

This chapter is all about preparation. Nothing on earth beats good preparation. I'm not talking about spending an hour writing questions. I'm talking about backing everything up with research: you want to know what you're talking about, be relevant, and not ask the same thing that everybody else has talked about.

But first, let's talk about nerves.

There are a few things that cause you to feel nervous about talking to bands in an interview situation In my experience, these nerves come from a few common places. These are awe, standards you need or want to meet, a lack of knowledge, and the possibility of talking to a recalcitrant interviewee.

1. Awe

If you're a fan of a band or musician, then this is going to be your biggest thing. My most nerve-wracking interview was the first time I talked to Rob Halford. But on examination, the nerves were equal parts awe, and equal parts of the second—standards. Dealing with awe-inspired nerves is perhaps the most difficult; all you can do is remind yourself that these people have been doing their thing for a really long time, that they are still people, and that manners and good preparation goes a very long way with other professionals. Think of yourselves as colleagues—because that's how it often pans out.

2. Standards—set by yourself or by others.

If you are interviewing a band or musician that's been around for a long time, then you're going to be nervous about meeting standards. In all likelihood, you are never going to be able to ask a question they have never been asked before—but you should strive to be as original as possible at all times, without getting weird, nasty, or just plain stupid. See also point (1) about awe.

3. Lack of knowledge.

You don't need to be a total geek regarding a band or genre in order to conduct an excellent interview; in fact, sometimes it can help if you're not. But if you don't have a great deal of knowledge, which can come as much from not knowing a band from a bar of soap, as not having heard enough of their back-catalogue, then it can make you nervous as hell. Happily, there is a way around it: good research.

4. A recalcitrant interviewee (in-interview).

This largely comes down to interview technique, and a certain mindfulness—but this will be addressed in later.

Dealing with nerves can be hard. But it is something that you can use to your advantage. If you are nervous, it is a strong signal to you that you need to take action of some kind; becoming engaged in the interview process is one of the best ways of dealing with that nervousness. However, the nerves you experience immediately prior to an interview—that is, in the five minutes before a phone call takes place—can really only be dealt with by being properly set up, having checked that everything works, and breathing deeply.

Always remember that interviews, at their best, are good conversations. That is really what you should be aiming for: a good, engaging, two-way conversation that you can remember fondly.

Preparation makes a good interview great

Is it the interview method, or the questions themselves? Well, these are both important—but what makes a good interview great is the amount of research you put into it beforehand.

There are some very basic, bog-standard things you can do when you are preparing to interview a band. Ever heard the phrase "break down the elephant"? Below is a step-by-step to help you prepare effectively.

Determine whether the interview is regarding a new release, or a tour, or both. If it's about a release—make sure you get a copy, or at least one rough-cut—to listen to, so you at least have a vague sense of it beforehand. Never be afraid to ask for samples. If it's about a tour, you need to find all of the details about that tour, and as much information/reviews on the previous tour, if possible

Read as much about the history of the band as possible. Given the pervasive nature of the internet, this is so much easier now than it was ten or more years ago. Find the official biography, the label's biography (if you have access to it), fans' details of the band, and so on. The bio will give you a way of attacking the interview. Some artists, like Bumblefoot, have a really personal bio; others have very little at all.

Read as many news items of the band as possible, from a diverse range of places. What you are looking for is a key piece of information that is unusual, striking, or odd. These things are great conversation topics. For example, Rob Cavestany collects amphibians; cue endless excitement about this on his part prior to their last tour of Australia with their original lineup.

Find the band's discography, and get familiar with it. Do any live albums stand out? Any split releases that stand out? Any artwork that is striking? What did the early material sound like compared to the new (if you have access to it)? Doing this will likely cause small items to stand out on their own, as being worthwhile of bringing up in conversation.

Read reviews of all releases. This will enable you to get a sense of how the band has progressed, what the major issues have been for fans and media in the past, and what expectations are like for the new release. This should give you some material to consider asking.

Get as many additional details on a release as possible. Think about guest appearances, who the producer was, where it was recorded, where it was mixed, who did the artwork, who the engineer was, what the early promo has been like. This enables you to find out what the team that the band worked with was like. How was the art created and how much input did they have, and so on.

Get as many details on a band's tour cycle as possible. Some bands tour not much, others tour for three years at continuously, before having a break and going back into the studio. Some bands write and record in their tour buses. It's rich material for finding out how they cope, and how much effort they put in for their fans. Some bands, for example, have a really good family that helps them through; others rely on alcohol to blast their way through a tour; still others have small things—like an interest in architecture—that keep them interested when they're on the road continually.

Read other people's interviews with the person or band you will be speaking with. This is perhaps the most vital thing you can do, because it gives you a sense of what the person or band is like to talk to (talkative or otherwise) and how he or she responds to certain questions. It gives you a sense of personality, so you can prepare yourself mentally; and it gives you a really good idea of the types of questions that other people are asking, what to avoid, what might be good to know more about, and so on. This can really help you with your interview framework.

Take care over your interview questions

It is important to take care over your interview questions, because your questions will frame your interview. In the first instance you want to make sure you cover the ground you need to; in the second, you want to eliminate closed (yes/no) questions; and in the third instance, you want to ensure that the questions flow well, or at least tell some sort of story on their own.

While you can bang up a set of standardised interview questions upon which to base all future interviews, I don't recommend it. It can give you a good framework, sure, but at the same time, all of your interviews end up sounding the same, coming from the same perspective. It also means that you run the risk of being stereotyped—something which I suggest is good to avoid. Having a new set of questions for every band also helps you to remain memorable: never forget that bands are friends with other bands, and do actually talk to each other. Yes, they do talk about interviews, especially if you are interviewing all major bands on a tour cycle together.

If you can get to the point where major musicians with a big history tell you that your interview was awesome—three months after said interview took place—then you've hit your mark. No, it's not impossible: this happened to me in early 2009, and you could've knocked me over with a feather. Take from this a good lesson: you're far better off being humble and professional, than caring about syndicated writings. If you get a reputation as an excellent journalist among the bands first, then the industry will hear about you from those bands, meaning you're more likely to go the distance.

How to pull your notes into interview questions

Like everything, there is a simple method to writing interview questions. The key is getting the method right for yourself, and engaging in it religiously. It takes a while to find the method, if you're searching for it on your own. Here is a starting point for you:

1. Sketch out everything that you want to know about or talk about

2. Write out all those points as single questions. Don't double-up unless you have to—meaning, the second part should ask for an expansion on the first part: part two should never be a second question

3. Make sure all your questions are individual questions

4. Make sure all your questions are open—that is, they don't require 'yes' or 'no' responses

5. Make sure they flow nicely—that is, think of all the possible interactions between yourself and the interviewee arising from each

question. Reorder your questions until the imagined interview flows smoothly

6. Read the questions aloud to see if they flow nicely when spoken (need I mention that this is vital if you're doing the interview by phone?). If you stumble, rework and practise!

7. Critically analyse how many questions you have, and cull where necessary

8. Re-order until you're happy.

If you end up with more than thirteen interview questions, refine them. Most interviews run for an absolute maximum of twenty allowed minutes (especially by phone), so you need to make sure you can cover what you need to in the allowable time frame. If you have too many questions, and you haven't considered possible diversions, then you end up in a situation where you either ignore conversational threads (which are often very interesting) or you follow them and don't get the information you want. This is why having a small, precise list of questions, which allow for expansion or diversion, is important.

The reverse is also true, though. If you have a recalcitrant interviewee—one who is not particularly forthcoming—then you may need to think very quickly to get some engagement happening if your questions are too limited.

Set, and strive to meet, high standards. Always.

If you approach all parts of your journalism work with professionalism, those with whom you interact will respect it. While you might be nervous about meeting the high standards of other journalists in the field, you can literally only ever strive to meet the highest standards possible. If you make this something you do consciously all the time, then you will naturally float to the top of the pile.

Some people feel that there is a culture of elitism in the music industry—and especially in metal—which is justified. It doesn't mean that anybody who works in the field as a journalist should feel overwhelmed by it, or put upon because of it. Instead, it's a challenge for you to meet a very high standard; that challenge is a worthy one, and one that calls for all of your knowledge of the art, and all of your professional flexibility.

It doesn't matter whether you're a student, a volunteer, a staff writer, or a paid freelancer: you must always strive to meet high standards. A solid method, a good framework, and a clear knowledge of what you're doing and why, will go a long way. You can always skip steps in each part of the way, but if you do, you need to remember that you are also eroding the foundations that support your work. 10. Interviews: Running the show As you've seen in chapter nine, preparing for an interview can be time-consuming. Good preparation will, however, stand you in good stead, ensure you look like the pro you are aiming to be, and will help to settle those nerves down.

Running on from this, the present chapter will go through the nitty-gritties of actually conducting the interview itself: how to ask questions, how to deal with talkative interviewees (and the converse, the monosyllabic), and how to focus on both the interview and the conversation without falling to pieces in the process.

Rather than examining all types of interviews at once, which is confusing for both of us, I'm going to look exclusively at telephone interviews. This is because the majority of interviews one does are conducted over the phone. Chapter 11 will go into emailer interviews (known as 'emailers'), and how they differ in practise to a 'phoner'. I'm not going to get into the face-to-face interview, because you should be able to take the everything about phoners and turn it into a F2F quite easily. You might, in fact, have greater trouble disengaging, but that is part and parcel of a good conversation.

Immediately prior to the interview

First things first: make absolutely sure that you know what time the interview is scheduled to take place, and what your time allocation is. In my case, all of my interview times come through as Australian Eastern time (standard or daylight time); not being in that time zone, I have to make sure that I know that I have the right time. Knowing how long you've got will help you stay on time so you don't put anybody else out. It helps, for the purposes of small-talk, to find out the day and time in which the person you'll be talking to is currently existing. I recall talking to the legendary Mickey Dee straight after he'd come off-stage, full of the high and adrenaline of a live performance. Knowing these sorts of details will prompt you to keep it quick, stretch it out, talk about the weather or the people, or whatever else is going on.

The second thing you need to make absolutely sure of is whether the band is calling you, or whether you are calling them. If the latter, ensure that you have any relevant phone card details provided by the label, agent, distro, or whatever agency is scheduling the interviews, and make sure that the phone number—and any required PINs or passwords—is correct. If the band is calling you, make sure that you are in the right place, with the right phone. Trust me, there's nothing worse than being prepared for a recorded interview and having poor facilities, and then facing the prospect of typing the transcript as you go.

To this end, if you are doing this from home, make sure that nobody else is on the phone when you need to use it, or when a band needs to call you. It's a simple thing to word people up ahead of time: so simple that it's something easily overlooked.

The third thing you need to do is make sure that your recording facilities function properly, that you have your questions at the ready, and the right version of those questions. Also try to make sure that the room you're in is quiet enough for you to get a good recording; having to work from a poor recording will make your write-up process much more work than it needs to be. Besides, you might want to keep your recording in an archive.

And finally, grab yourself a glass of water or a cup of coffee. If you're nervous, coffee's probably not a good idea—but if it's early in the morning, as some interviews inevitably are, it can be no end of help in waking yourself up.

Kicking the interview off

So—you're all set up. Now what? The phone rings, or is ringing, and your heart is thumping like mad. Here's a tip for when you answer (or the band answers at the other end): keep an ear on your own voice. It is a truism that using your 'best voice' at all times makes nearly everything better. To this end, ensure that you are speaking clearly, slowly and naturally. If you are smiling, so much the better! You might feel like a right tosser, but the smile does come through in your voice. Keep the pace relaxed and be in it to enjoy yourself.

Engaging in small talk at the beginning of an interview is not a bad thing at all, unless it starts to eat into your interview time. Small talk can be a fabulous way of getting the measure of your interviewee: some are all business-business-business; some have just woken up; some are rushing around organising and buying things in the madness of pre-tour; some have been pulled out of the studio. You're talking to people at the other end who have busy lives, and sometimes this 'busyness' can intrude into the interview situation. Being able to have a bit of a chat about nothing in particular will help you to scope what the environment is like at the other end.

To give context to this, one interview I did started out with the band member at the other end of the phone (in Sweden, I think) sounding sleepy. He was making coffee, and started asking what the weather was like. He told me that he 'just needed to talk shit for a while' so that he could wake up and get into the business side of things. If you ever find yourself in this sort of situation, it's clue for you to relax and get to know someone. Don't be in a rush to get into your questions straight away.

Getting into the 'human side' of your interviewee is vital: but I'll get to that later.

Asking questions, and letting your interviewee talk

If you have engaged in small talk, however briefly, with the person at the other end, you will find yourself (hopefully) naturally segueing into your first question. If you struggle, a good thing to do is to thank them for their time before you start and tell them roughly how many questions you've got. If nothing else, this gives your interviewee some context for the interview that's about to take place, and it also gives them a time framework.

If you haven't really spoken on the phone down an international line before, it is well to remember that there is often a delay between what you say and when your interviewee hears it, and vice versa. If your interviewee is on a mobile phone, then that delay can be a lot longer. Some countries are worse than others, too: Australia to Britain can be immediate; Australia to Sweden or Finland can have a palpable two or three second delay; Australia to the US or Canada can swing either way.

The lesson here is: don't be so eager to get the interview done that you're tripping over what your interviewee is trying to say. I could tell you that it's unprofessional, but the reality of it is that it's just downright uncomfortable. If it happens throughout an interview, then there's a good chance you'll wish a big black hole would just open up and swallow you whole.

It is important to let your interviewee talk. If you've done your research right, and have crafted some nice questions, then there is a very good chance that the person at the other end will have to think about what to say before saying it. An interviewee who has to think is engaging fully in what you're asking, and it's a sign of a good question. If your questions are getting answers that sound suspiciously like they were prepared ahead of time, your warning bells should start ringing! It means you will have to change your style on the fly. The last thing you want is the same interview as hundreds of other journalists all around the world.

Dealing with Mr Business & the recalcitrant interviewee

Yes, they exist: band members for whom interviews are work, and therefore should be conducted in the most militaristic, business-like way possible. Such a band member is often characterised by answers to most questions prepared ahead of time (and delivered a million times in the same way); an unwillingness to engage in small talk; a brisk voice; and a rapid-fire answer delivery.

Recalcitrant interviewees may not come from the same place, but they are incredibly difficult to get talking. The recalcitrant interviewee will prefer to answer your questions with monosyllabic answers (even open-ended questions will elicit but a brief response); they may come across as being annoyed or irritated; they will have a low tolerance for small talk; they may sound tired, or jaded, or like they'd rather just be elsewhere. Forcing yourself to engage in this type of interaction can be unbelievably hard work.

So what do you do in this situation? The answer is so simple, it's beyond belief: try to get them to laugh (without telling a joke or otherwise going beyond your immediate boundaries). It might simply be a matter of commenting on something they've said, which then makes it seem like the interviewee has a sense of humour.

Getting a laugh out of a business-like or recalcitrant interviewee is like spinning magic: it turns them back into people. All of a sudden their approach becomes warmer and more relaxed, and the 'interview' turns into a conversation.

Interviews as conversations, and particular technique

The best interviews are the ones that are two-way conversations that you can remember fondly, and that you come out of feeling like you've made a new good friend. Unsurprisingly, conversational interviews are the ones from which you will obtain a higher percentage of golden material.

Conversational interviews, like many things, all comes down to skill and a mastery of technique. On the one hand you need to ask the questions you want answers to; on the other hand, you want to be able to follow the conversation. How do you do this?

Easy: treat it like a normal conversation. Your questions are markers that segment the conversation, and between those you are able to follow the threads of what comes up as it comes up, unless you are constrained by time limits. Be wary, however, of simply asking more questions. If you have structured your questions properly, your frame will provide boundaries and markers almost perfectly, and allow you to segue from one topic of conversation to the next.

As with any good conversational technique, you need to show that you're listening: this means providing comments about what the interviewee says, making affirmative noises occasionally, and also adding a bit of information of your own before following up the conversational hook, and leaving it to the interviewee to run with it.

What you find when you move from questions to comments is a deeper level of engagement, and the interviewee will often be more forthcoming with more interesting information. It's not a 'trick' of interrogation: it is a way of enabling both parties to forget that this is a structured, formal discussion, and that it's more like one between friends.

What you find, when you engage in a discussion like this, is that it is sad to have to whiz through the remainder of your questions, and it is terrible to have to end a conversation.

Bringing band members to the level of the 'human' is vital if you are going to forge good connections, establish good rapport, and bring your interview out of the formal and into the conversational. However, on some occasions it can also work against you.

Dealing with the talkative interviewee

Sometimes you find yourself in the situation where the interviewee—because you've let them talk—goes on, and on, and on, and on. I sometimes find myself so amused that I let them go on, just to see if they'll stop; often they don't. Usually, for an interviewee like this, the only way to stop the flow is to intervene.

Learning how to intervene is vital if you don't have the leisure of time, and you are constrained by other journalists who are slotted into the schedule behind you. If you're not off the phone on time, it means you are putting somebody else out, and that's just bad grace. Not to mention that when it happens with ten journalists, and you're the last one on the list, you might be running up to an hour and a half behind.

Realistically, there's no particularly graceful way of dealing with an over-talkative interviewee, except for shaving your questions down as you go, so that there is something specific he or she has to answer. Then, if you have to interrupt, do it by way of commenting on what they said, and segueing nicely into your next question at the same time. If your questions have been structured well, then this will not be particularly difficult for you to do. It's really just awkward and practise makes perfect—as with everything.

Keeping your mind in two places at once, without falling over

Following the flow of a conversation, and following your interview list, isn't quite as difficult as it may sound. Here are some tips that can help you.

If you're recording directly onto your computer, turn everything else but your recording software off. Don't look at Facebook, or any other social network for that matter, while you're interviewing someone; don't check your emails; don't do anything else. Focus on what you're doing right now: it's so much easier.

Print out your questions list and put a line through each question as it's been answered. This can help you enormously if your interviewee is talkative, and answering questions ahead of time. It can also help you to reorder questions quickly if you feel that the conversation is taking things in a slightly different direction.

Keep a scrap of paper next to you and jot down anything that occurs to you to ask, as the conversation goes on. Sometimes it happens that something an interviewee says is so enormously interesting that you think, 'I must ask about that'—and then you forget what it was. Writing a note or two down will help you to remember. This can also help you follow the flow of conversation even better.

Don't think about your questions to the exclusion of the interviewee. It's really awkward: I've done it. You end up facing a gap where the interviewee has clearly just asked you something that you have totally missed and need to find a good way around as an excuse.

And last but not least, something to confuse you completely. If necessary, focus on the conversation, to the exclusion of your notes. It's the conversation that matters, because it's the conversation, not your notes, that is going to generate your article.

7. INTERVIEWS

Emailers are Different

In chapter 6, we looked at how to prepare for interviews, and how to prepare yourself for them. Well, for phoners, that is. We looked at a whole range of things, including interview technique, conversations, dealing with Mr Business, and how to stay focused.

Comparatively, email-based interviews (which we call *emailers*, as opposed to *phoners*) are easier in some ways; but they can also be far more maddening.

And so, the first frequently-asked question: Do emailer interview questions need to be different? The short answer is: Yes.

Sorry to disappoint you. Absolutely, yes, your emailer questions will differ —or should!—to your phoner questions. Once you work out your interviewing style, however, you will be able to short-cut the process of writing questions.

All you have do to, once you've mastered the ability to write good telephone interview questions, is tailor them for an email format.

While getting a good interview over the phone comes down to interview technique and—although I hate to say it—the quality of your voice (such as in how you project yourself, how relaxed you sound, and how prepared you are), you could strip the requirements for what makes a 'good interview' by email down to two things, and two things only.

These are:

1. good questions

2. having a person at the other end who is relaxed, has time to reply, and is reasonably good at expressing him- or herself in writing.

The second point is one that you can do very little about, and is something over which you have absolutely no control. The first one, however, can influence the second. Good questions will make replying less of a chore; if it's less of a chore, then you will gain better answers by default.

How to write good emailer interview questions

You already know how to write interview questions; but let's revisit a portion of Chapter 6. The information and advice there is as applicable here as anywhere.

How to pull your notes into interview questions

1. Sketch out everything that you want to know about or talk about

2. Write out all those points as single questions. Don't double-up unless you have to—meaning, the second part asks for an expansion on the first part: it should never be a second question

3. Make sure all your questions are individual questions

4. Make sure all your questions are open—that is, they don't require just 'yes' or 'no' responses

5. Make sure they flow nicely—that is, think of all the possible interactions between yourself and the interviewee arising from each question. Reorder your questions until the interview flows smoothly

6. Read the questions aloud to see if they flow nicely when spoken (need I mention that this is vital if you're doing the interview by phone?)

7. Critically analyse how many questions you have, and cull where necessary

8. Re-order until you're happy.

Remember these? Right about now, you are wondering how some of these are even relevant, such as number 6. To this, I merely have to say: if you can read the question aloud without tripping over, then your punctuation is correct, and your reader will have less trouble.

Let's imagine that you have your list of questions in front of you. Here is a very simple step-by-step for tweaking them into email format.

1. Keep your series of questions focused.

Go through your list again, and keep yourself to 10 questions or less. My best interviews, for instance, have been done on between five and eight questions, regardless of format. Regardless of this, I firmly believe that keeping to a basic 10 questions looks like only a few, keeps your interview focused on what is important, and enables you to engage in a write-up that isn't overly long or arduous.

2. Ask yourself whether the questions could be answered without clarification.

In a telephone interview situation, your interviewee has the luxury of being able to ask you what you mean if he or she doesn't quite get it. This can prove essential for people from non-English speaking countries (and in metal, that's a LOT of bands). In an email interview situation, lack of understanding will result in lack of answers. You only have 10 questions to play with, so don't limit your material. If you are in doubt about anything, rewrite until you're happy.

3. Add contextual information.

Something that has quickly become my own rule of thumb is adding contextual information for your question when it goes out in an emailer, unless it is bleedingly obvious what you mean and what you're asking about. Don't be afraid to tell the person at the other end that you read on some website about [this], and your question is [that]. If anything, it proves how far you'll go to be as original as possible, and it gives your bland little email some character and personality.

4. Keep phrases short!

If you're writing an emailer for a person whose first language is not English, refer to point 2, and keep your sentences short as hell. Do not ramble on. Especially do not ramble on for two or three lines. Keep it short and sweet. Not only will this enable greater comprehension if the person's English is poor, but if he or she has to resort to language translators, then the software will cope far more admirably if you don't have a ton of phrases running into each other, separated only by commas.

5. Check, check, check, check, check.

Double-check, triple-check, and check again until you're happy. Remove any questions that could be answered too easily or stupidly (unless that's what you're after); avoid yes-no questions; make sure your spelling and punctuation are 100% perfect, and make sure that your language and tone are both pitched just right.

The difference between speech and writing

Most musicians are used to giving telephone interviews; it's just the way it's done, unless you happen to get lucky and get in on the ground, face-to-face. Sure, that's obvious, you might think. What might not be obvious is that most people are quite comfortable talking to somebody else. And yet, a lot of people freeze when they have to write anything.

Why this is the case is anybody's guess, but as a writer, editor and publisher myself, my firm belief is that it comes down to a person's childhood. At school, we're all told what's wrong with what and how we write, and are very rarely congratulated for it. Only suck-ups get the congratulations. We hear in the media all the time about how poor our literacy is, whether we're children or adults. Apparently, none of us can read, even fewer of us can write, and if you have the ability to write then you must be a Goddamned Genius. This perspective is not only untrue, it has given nearly everybody a complex.

So with this in mind, you have to remember that if your interviewee is not particularly comfortable in writing, you should be prepared for a returned interview that might not meet your expectations.

You will receive very short responses, or very long responses. The spelling will nearly always be patchy, same with punctuation. Sometimes multiple band members reply, each taking a different question. Sometimes, you get 'yes/no' answers to open-ended questions. Sometimes you get interviews returned with only half of the questions filled in. Sometimes you just get smart-arse replies. But in the main, if you present your material right, you'll get approximately the same volume (words-wise) of response as has gone into the question.

The worst thing is that there's not much you can do about that sort of thing, even with the best preparation. Regardless, prepare yourself mentally for it, just in case what you get back is likely to throw you into Dismal Swamp.

Other factors to consider about emailers

There are a few other factors about emailers that you'll want to consider. Following is a short, snappy list to round off the chapter.

If you get the opportunity to start right at the beginning with your music journalism, go for phoners first. This will help you test-run your questions and technique in person. You can tell an awful lot about how prepared you really are by the demeanour of the person on the other end of the line. It's more nerve-wracking, but it's better for your development in the long-run.

Think about the format of your email, and never assume everybody runs a Mac or that everybody runs Windows. If you're sending an attachment, make sure it's a Rich Text File (*.rtf) because RTFs are multi-platform and run without any trouble. Usually.

It can be tempting to write little notes in an email, sucking up to a band, gushing about them or to them, or otherwise getting into fan boy or groupie territory. For the love of god, DON'T do this. It is good to include a note at the beginning thanking the interviewee for their time, and noting that you know how much longer emailers take than phone interviews. That's it. Gush is just disgusting.

You don't have the luxury of following the conversation, so your questions need to be as full and insightful (and open-ended) as possible, and they need to flow one into another easily and logically.

You might not get the interview back for a long time, especially if your questions are convoluted, despite trying repeatedly. The person at the other end could be tired, busy, not giving a shit, or even pissed off that he or she has to do it in writing, and this might affect what he or she writes, or their attitude in general. Remember this if what you receive is not what you had hoped for.

You might well get monosyllabic responses, to even the most open-ended questions, and not be able to use any of it. Thankfully, it's pretty rare.

Your interviewee, despite all your best efforts, may totally misunderstand what you mean, and answer a question you haven't asked (when this happens, it's not usually something you wanted or needed to know).

8. WRITING UP

Part One: The Feature Article

Now that you have your skills down in actually doing interviews, it's time for the realisation that your work is only two-thirds done. Now it's time to learn how to pull it all together. This is where your writing skills are vital, and why I've always stated that the best music journos are writers first, and fans last.

Writing anything always comes down to purpose and audience. Without a strong sense of purpose, your writing will wander; without a strong sense of audience, anything you write will fail to hit the mark with your readers.

To some extent, music journalists and critics have it fairly easy because they always write for a defined audience, and, usually, they have a defined purpose. The purpose will often be explained to you when the interview is confirmed. Most of the time, it is to promote a new album, or a forthcoming tour. Such interviews easily comprise 90% of a music journalist's work.

The daunting thing for metal music journos is knowing that vast numbers of metal fans are very much metal geeks, and will generally have some sort of criticism about your work. This is yet another reason why doing your research is so vitally important, particularly if you are not incredibly familiar with a band.

Be aware, that if you're not a metal geek, you can still producing incredible work, provided that your research is tight, and that you set high standards for yourself.

Good writing skills, as I mentioned above, are vitally important. One of the 'standard' formats for interviews in metal journalism, which you see online and in print—one that annoys me—is the regular old Q & A style 'write-up'. If I'm going to be perfectly honest, to me a Q&A is not a write-up at all: it's cheating. And it's cheating because all you have to do is plug responses into your questions. No thought goes into it whatsoever. It is not journalistic work in the slightest; a monkey could do it.

Of course, Q & A formats do have a place (see the next chapter). But at the same time, they aren't as interesting to read, and they don't force the writer to think or to use all (or any) of the information he or she gained during the research stage.

One of the benefits of writing a full-length feature is that it gives you the opportunity to show your readers the personality of the interviewee. This is conveyed through how you represent their speech, the comments you make along the way, and any surrounding context that the feature article allows you. For instance, you might interview someone who is rushing around doing pre-tour tasks while talking to you on their mobile phone, or who was driving somewhere interesting on their way home from a studio or something; you can't use that information if you're just writing Q & As. In a feature, you can highlight where your interviewee was amused, or annoyed; you can explain where they were, you can use small talk and pre-interview conversation as one of the means of providing an insight into the person whom you are interviewing. You have so much more flexibility in terms of creating your story.

Musicians, of whatever level of fame, are just people. The best features give you an insight into that person; doing this well requires you to write clearly, concisely, and engagingly. This is why writers generally—whether they are writers of fiction or non-fiction—tend to produce outstanding work: good writers make people their study.

But first, onto the method for getting your interview material into a useful format.

To transcribe or not to transcribe: that is the question

If you're just starting out, it is a good idea to fully transcribe the recording of your interview, if you did it by phone or face-to-face. Once you've got a transcription, you pretty much have a plan—if your questions were structured well enough—that will guide you in how to structure your feature article. Emailers are easier in the sense that they completely cut out this transcription step of the work. Of course, the trade-off in the latter is that you have something completely devoid of emotion (and sometimes personality).

One of the benefits of transcription is that you can start to think about the best placement for your material. You are able to print off the transcription, in order to work out which parts of the interview you want to use as direct quotes, which as paraphrase, and which as additional commentary or contextual information. Being able to scribble on your transcription to make notes for such a purpose can be highly beneficial.

If you've been doing this sort of thing for a while, it is natural that you will begin to work directly from the recordings: you'll have the experience behind you that gives you the ability to know instinctively which material works as supporting info, and which parts to use as quotation.

But—in the beginning—*always* transcribe. It takes longer, but the skills it provides you with are invaluable.

Remember you are writing a story

All features are a story, in the same way that a piece of fiction is a story: it features a character (your interviewee), engaged in a particular subject (your purpose, generally an album or tour), and you need to write it in an engaging way, filled with expression and quotation (and dialogue, too, if you feel it fits).

To some extent, the structure of your interview questions will dictate the structure of your story; once you've analysed your transcript, you'll know how the story will flow best, and which parts of it will be most engaging if they are presented directly.

The notes that you made during your research will provide you with good background information, and will hopefully be verified or fleshed out by your interviewee. Engaging with the readers, generally fans of a band, is important: therefore if something is common knowledge amongst fans you can point out that fans will know X or Y, and you can go on to explain it for others who may not be *au fait* with that information. Never *ever* assume that every reader is a fan. Casual fans are just as important target audiences; in some cases, more so: on tour cycles, sometimes it's the casual fans who can make or break a particular show financially, depending on whether or not they decide to go.

The inverted pyramid mode of writing: put the most important things first

There is a type of writing mode, known well to those who studied communication or technical writing at a tertiary level, known as the 'inverted pyramid mode'. This mode of writing dictates that a summary of the most important information should always appear at the beginning of a piece of writing, with the remainder flowing on from it.

In some ways, it is well to remember this when writing feature articles. However, if you write for a publication or blog online, then generally this is dictated to you anyway, through the need for a title and a teaser, and then the body of the article afterwards. Those field requirements that you have to fill in are themselves dictated by the best structure for on-screen copy.

In print, such a structure is not defined by others on your behalf. If you find yourself writing for print, it is well worth keeping in mind that a strong feature will generally include some type of 'summary' at the top. But always be careful when you write them. It is one thing to write an abstract of an article, and something entirely different to write an engaging introduction that summarises the who, what, where, and why of what you're writing.

When you find yourself in this position, always go for the engaging introduction, rather than a bland summary or abstract of an article. Why? In the first instance, you want to draw your readers in rather than put them off. In the second instance, it's easier to write than a clinical or abstruse manifestation of what you've otherwise done. In the third instance, writing an engaging introduction can be done at the start rather than at the end of what you write, provided, of course, that you revisit it when you finish the feature to make sure that it is a true reflection of what you've written.

Important things to remember

1. Paraphrase to create prose.

The material that you have from your interviewee, which you are not using as direct quotes, is not—contrary to what many people think—wasted material. This is where your richest material will, in fact, come from: you can paraphrase it, change it around, and use the information you have gained from the interview as part of what you are writing. It is perfectly legitimate to do this, provided you don't get it wrong. If you have done sufficient research ahead of time, then what you gain ought to verify what you already know.

2. One sentence between quotes does not a feature article make.

Given that writing full features is an often arduous and difficult task, it becomes tempting at times (especially at busy times) to plonk in a series of quotes with some scant intervening material. This is not a feature article. It is a patchwork of quotes, held together by the thinnest of connective tissues. If you don't have time to write the feature properly, negotiate with whoever you are writing for, for an extra day. Going the extra distance to knit together a powerful article is better for your career, and for your self-respect as a journalist, than is turning in something that is on time but substandard.

3. Your article should have a natural sense of rhythm and flow.

If your article's constituent parts do not flow on from each other seamlessly, and if you are not drawn to read on from one part to the next, then your article has been poorly put together. If on a re-read you find yourself drawn inextricably from the beginning to the end, however, you will know that you've done a good job. Keep an eye on the rhythm of the piece and on how it segues from one part to the next. If it jolts or is gappy, do whatever you can to fix it.

4. Restructuring quotes is acceptable.

Sometimes when you transcribe your recording, you will find that parts of some answers to questions are follow-on comments from material or issues previously discussed. In this situation, if you want to use it as a direct quote, you are better off shuffling the material around and putting the same material together—and this is perfectly acceptable, provided you quote accurately.

5. Be careful of making assumptions.

If you find that your interviewee is tired, speaks as though he or she is homesick (especially on tour), or there is something else that piques your interest, be *very* wary of writing it as though it is fact. You are better off, if you find yourself in this situation, to leave any comments like that out of your write-up. Instead, file it in the back of your mind as something to ask as an additional question the next time you find yourself in a similar situation, and get the information directly: you might be wrong about what you're hearing otherwise. If you do write an assumption as fact, it is feasible that you'll find yourself at the mercy of a very pissed off musician who requests amendments or, worse, that the entire article be pulled—thereby displeasing your editor and/or your publisher. It's happened to me once, and once is enough. You learn very quickly from such mistakes.

6. When it's finished, put your article aside and go back to it to proof and re-read later.

One of the most important things you can do when you're writing features (or writing anything destined for publication) is to set the finished product aside once it's done. If you can, let it lie fallow for a minimum of 24 hours, and don't think about it at all during that time. It is incredibly valuable to go back to it with fresh eyes after a break, because you will pick up errors in spelling and grammar, places where the flow is broken or inconsistent, and areas that you know can be rephrased or tightened up. This will especially be the case with your introduction.

7. When you think the article's finished, read it aloud.

Yes, you need to read it aloud, and yes you will feel like a right tosser reading your work aloud to yourself. However, this will give you the final insight into flow, and into grammatical and punctuation errors. If, when you read your work aloud, you stumble, have to re-read parts, or it otherwise doesn't 'feel right', you know that those areas are the ones that you need to go back and fix.

9. WRITING UP
Part Two: Effective Q & A Pieces

My perspective on feature articles, presented in the foregoing chapter, is all well and good. But sometimes you are required to produce a Q & A (question-and-answer) piece for a publication. Some publications will not publish interviews in any other format.

With this in mind, therefore, I must include some material on creating effective Q & A articles.

The key word here is 'effective'. Nearly anybody can string together a page of questions, plonk into it the responses to those questions, give it a quick proof-read, and send it off to an editor. And nearly everybody who writes question-and-answer pieces does exactly this. They are 'effective' insomuch as they do exactly what they say they will do: provide you questions asked, and answers given. But they do nothing to assist in the readability of the work itself.

A good Q & A piece is as much a story as is a feature article. What you lose in flexibility and overt contextualisation, you gain in directness of interaction. Even if you have to present your interview in this format, try not to be tempted to let go of the story.

Looking back at your interview questions—and the responses, if you've transcribed your interview already—you'll quickly be able to see whether or not it tells a story. As discussed *ad infinitum* in the foregoing chapters, a good set of questions will tend to drive the creation of a story anyway.

One of the most important things to remember with your Q & A is that it is not necessarily the interaction that makes the interview interesting, but the framework. The framework in this case is manufactured from a good, insightful introduction that sets the scene; a good flow of questions and responses that culminate a peak of sorts towards the end; and a good conclusion and overview at the end. Give your Q & A the environment that it requires if it's going to shine.

Stand back and reconfigure things

1. Take yourself out of the equation.

The old question-and-answer format is so much like a transcript of an interview that it is tempting to include interjections by the interviewer, or interviewer comments and commentary designed to keep an interview flowing. For the sanity of your readers, and for your own credibility, never ever do this. It looks completely amateurish, and distracts the reader from what is important (i.e. the interviewee, not you).

The best way to scale things back is to print out your transcript and go through it with a pencil. Aside from any relevant emotional interjections that you may have scripted in, such as *[laughs]*, strike out all of your own interjections, any commentary that is not integral to the interview, as well as anything else that can be dispensed with.

2. Group and restyle for story flow.

Next, choose a different colour pencil, and group your questions and answers until you have a nice little story-like flow. You might find, for example, that answers to some questions on similar topics are better put together as though other questions were never asked. You might find that some of your off-the-cuff intervening questions or comments are better than the original questions, and you might want to use those instead.

3. What you want is the pot of gold.

Now you think I'm mad: *what pot of gold?* This lies in the gaps you identify through the process. The gaps for which you do not have a question, and to which you can find absolutely no way of segueing without adding a paragraph or two of context in between. This is where we come to the meat of our chapter.

Work to The Rule of Thirds

The Rule of Thirds is one I created. It says that you can provide meat and potatoes two-thirds of the time, but every so often you're going to want salad on the side, or cake. In other words, you want the meat of the interview two-thirds of the time, and creation of story for the remaining third.

While most Q & A format interviews do not provide contextualising paragraphs, this is not to say that you can't. In fact, it is preferable that you provide some respite from the interview itself, and give the reader some additional information. It's a lot better than ploughing through something that is effectively a disjointed read.

Always remember that your task is to bring your interviewee and his or her fans more closely together. A disjointed article is never going to assist with that bond, because it puts up a wall between your text and the person reading it.

Of note, though, is that your average Q & A is flexible enough that you can go almost half-way between your feature article and a plain list of questions and answers.

Have a look at your interview transcript, after you've gone through and eliminated some parts and combined others. Let's say that this leaves you with about nine questions, with some introductory and concluding remarks on either side of it.

This gives you the luxury of providing three sets of questions and answers, and a chunk of intervening prose—three times. If your transcript has a decent structure, but not one that you would rely on and would consider absolutely water-tight in terms of flow, you could break your transcript into themes, and create intervening material to smooth out the borders of each thematic part.

The added paragraphs needn't be too long. They might be merely four lines each. But if they are well crafted, then you will find yourself submitting a Q & A with a bit of sparkle and class.

Important things to remember

The important things to remember for Q & A articles are similar to those for feature articles. All of the points about flow, spelling, punctuation, reading aloud, making assumptions, and so on, are just as relevant here as anywhere. Therefore, I am not going to repeat myself; though I do encourage you to review them (see the end of Chapter 8).

1. You are not important, the interviewee is.

All of us seek fame and glory in one form or another, which is why it's so difficult to write yourself out of question-and-answer interviews. Nobody wants to read about your laughter, your "listening" noises, your inane commentary. Take them all out. Great interviews, from the reader's perspective, are those that impart a lot of good information. They don't point out the nervousness or perceived self-importance of the journalist.

2. Q & A interviews still need to tell a story.

Whatever you write, you need to tell a story. Your Q & A might feel like the easy way through to a published "feature" piece, one without the pain, but if it doesn't tell a story then you are selling yourself, the publication, and your readers short. Give us a sense of story through creation of good flow. If you follow the Rule of Thirds, you'll find that this happens a little more naturally.

3. Spelling and punctuation are important.

Even though the Q & A interview write-up is rather more informal than its feature article sister, the basic rules about good writing still apply. Fix your own errors—all of them. And fix any errata apparent in the interviewee's responses, too. It's all good fun imagining that Swedes put 's' on the end of every second word, but it makes for bloody hard reading. Unless your interviewee has an idiosyncrasy that is identifiable and unique—and is not just the result of speaking or writing a second or third language—do them a favour and clean up their words. Just never change the meaning; *that* is unforgiveable.

PRO-TIP #1
Be Careful of the One-Sheet

One-sheets are less common now than they used to be, but if you've worked as a journalist in the music industry, you would know exactly what I'm talking about when I refer to a one-sheet. If you don't know what a one-sheet is, here's a definition taken from Wikipedia:

> "In music publicity and distribution, a one-sheet is exactly what the name implies: One sheet of paper, on which information is provided about the musician and/or a specific release which is being distributed. One-sheets often accompany a record or CD when it is being shipped to radio stations and music publications (i.e., magazines, Web-based forums, etc.) A one-sheet is sometimes also referred to as a press sheet or a promo sheet."[20]

Other industries have one-sheets, too; but often they are simply sales pitches. In the music industry, this notion of 'selling' on a one-sheet is a lot less obvious, because of its tie-in with publicity.

A publicist once told me that when he worked for a major label there was often tension between marketing and publicity. Marketers have a penchant for saying to publicists: 'What I try to sell, you give away!'.

The notion that publicity is not selling, or is perhaps 'soft' selling, is bit of a white lie. The intention of publicists' work is to spread information about their bands and their bands' activities. What you will find, though, is that it is actually a sales pitch: the materials exist to help people provide good reviews and good press; to enable greater news reporting, thereby increasing the visibility of a label's 'product' (which is the band itself).

There is a second step to this sale, too. Through heightened visibility, and more reviews, you potentially generate higher sales. Through increased news reporting, you also gain heightened visibility in regards to tour dates: thereby potentially selling more tickets and more merchandise.

At its core, publicity is sales. It is unpaid advertising. It is marketing through generosity and useful, newsworthy information. And for critics who are reviewing materials, publicity often provides information about a release that they may not otherwise receive, thereby increasing a writer's understanding of what he or she is listening to. The more information you have, the better able you are to make an informed judgement; therefore your review will be more critical.

Right?

This is the understanding. But for those writers who are unschooled in rhetoric, a thinly veiled sales pitch in a one-sheet can exert undue influence on a review.

It is crucial for journalists and critics to realise that publicity materials are sales pitches, in whatever form they may take. Having written publicity material for bands myself, I know this intimately. Writing text for publicity purposes is exactly the same as writing text for sales, advertising, or press release purposes. It is merely framed differently.

Let's go look at rhetoric—because you'll need it! Rhetoric was originally one branch of the discipline of philosophy; it was a means for persuading a general audience using probable knowledge to resolve practical issues.

Aristotle defined rhetoric as the ability to see the available means of persuasion. When you deconstruct copy, you need to be able to see those means of persuasion, and determine how you are being persuaded by someone's writing.

This knowledge is useful not just in being careful about one-sheets. It is also useful for you in the general construction of your own writing. He who understands rhetoric can write anything, for anybody, and do it successfully. The trick is learning how to apply it.

I'm kind of going through these backwards, but following is a bit of a description of the three tools of rhetoric: *ethos, logos, pathos.*

Logos is reasoned argument, or 'argument from reason'. It is reasoned discourse, the ability to speak with clarity, logic, and reasonableness. It is what makes you appear prepared, and knowledgeable. *Logos* may be data, facts, figures, or the construing of such. Whatever it is that logically makes you look like you know what you are saying. In a one-sheet, we are looking at charting positions, numbers of tours, sales of albums, etc.

Pathos is the appeal to your audience's emotions; or, rather, to its sympathies and its imagination(s). *Pathos* is more refined that merely drawing an emotive response from your audience. It is the ability to tie that emotive response to your audience's empathies, to engage them well enough to imagine themselves (or someone close to them) in a particular situation. By tying the *pathos* to your audience—each audience member in turn—your work has a far greater persuasive appeal. In a one-sheet, *pathos* is found in a tendency towards a lot of adjectives that paint a picture of a band or its music, regardless of how accurate it may be.

Ethos is the most important of the three, which is why it is characteristically listed prior to the others. *Ethos* is an appeal to the honesty or authority of the speaker (or writer, or subject). While the persuader can provide a way into this, it is truly the audience that determines *ethos*. Drawing on *ethos* can be done in multiple ways:

By being a notable figure in the field in question, such as a producer, band member, high-profile musician, or an executive of a company whose business is that of the subject.

By having a vested interest in a matter, such as the person being related to the subject in question. By using impressive logos that shows to the audience that the speaker is knowledgeable on the topic.

By appealing to a person's ethics or character.

Now, go to a one-sheet you might have lying around and see if you can recognise the sales pitch in the copy. Look for words like *forefront, maturity, catchiness, simplicity, clear, sharp riffs*... How much of a dominating, positive spin does it have?

You can't argue that this is a bad thing, because everybody has to sell their products—in this day and age, more than ever. What you *can* argue is that one can be unduly influenced by this material before having heard the

77

album. Don't forget that one-sheets always accompany a release.

Back before the advent of online promo systems like Haulix, one-sheets would come folded in half, slipped into the front of a CD case; or sometimes hanging out of the top of a paper CD sleeve. You read them, went 'oh yeah', threw them on your desk, or table, or couch, or bench top. You only kept them if you found them valuable for some reason, like it contained a track listing that the CD didn't come with.

Now, however, things are different. You see this writing *every time* you log in to listen to those tracks on your Haulix account.

The key issue is that you (and your young critics, if you're an editor) are being pounded with positive spin.

Many unschooled reviewers (separate from critics; critics usually know what they're doing) drink in the one-sheet, like they drink in information about their favourite bands. Then they listen to the release, with the happy expectation that it will meet the levels insisted on by the one-sheet. Huge numbers of uncritical listeners cannot discern the difference between what they hear and what they've been told to hear, so you tend to get positive reviews from these cats... whether the album deserves it or not.

Not getting a one-sheet can sometimes be a godsend.

It is really nice to get releases without one-sheets occasionally, because you have to listen to the material and work really hard to decide on what you think is an appropriate response. It's not so much of a terrible thing, given there is the internet to assist with artwork, track listings, band compositions, and so on.

And, to be perfectly honest, the most useful material to a critic includes:

lyrics

art

visual artist

studio where recorded

who the producer(s) was/were

track listing

band composition

guest appearances

… and so on.

I would rather be able to give kudos (or the reverse) to specific people if I feel it is warranted: to artists who produce cover art and liner art; to producers who create great or shit sounds and mixes; to good (or otherwise) performances by guests. I would rather be able to come to my *own* understanding of an album through an entire package of art, lyrics, and music, and be able to talk to it knowledgeably, than to get some spin about where the band has come from. Because, honestly, who cares.

It is the *art* that is important. And 'art' is defined as the entire package when we talk about music. You cannot just take the music, because bands always make decisions on artwork and layout; and they often collaborate on lyrics, even when there is a primary lyricist. The lyrics are part and parcel of the music.

If you have a concept album, then nobody can argue that any part of it is unnecessary. Done right, the concept takes in visuals, words, music, and sometimes even videos.

Actively think whether to give your writers publicity material, if you have the choice.

If you are an editor, you need to consider whether to dole out publicity material, especially if you are mentoring and developing young writers.

It is sometimes necessary to provide budding critics with just the music and force them to hone their skills without the input of a publicist's carefully crafted text. It is vital to do it for critics whom one is mentoring, or whom one believes has a chance of being a critic or journalist of repute one day. It helps them to develop, and it helps you to publish quality content.

Withholding one-sheets can also sometimes be damaging. If you intend for your writer not only to review the album but to interview the band afterwards, he or she may well require the one-sheet. Why? Because usually the one-sheets provide valuable information—including, sometimes, quotes

—that other sources may not be able to provide.

A good journalist will scout existing press for interviews with a band he or she is set to interview, too, to gain information and to prevent mindless repetition of questions on the same album cycle; but sometimes the one-sheets will give you that little bit extra. There's no point asking stupid questions about **Tsjuder**'s 'album' *Atum Nocturnem* when it was an EP, for starters, and conceived as a demo as well.

If your writer does not know a band very well, the label's publicist can sometimes save them from looking like an idiot. I don't need to say that idiotic writers make publications look idiotic.

Whether you choose to use publicity materials you are provided (I like to refer to it as **the Force**, simply because if you don't watch out, you'll drown in them!) is largely a matter of personal discretion. Whether you train your writers to realise that publicity materials are sales materials is also up to you. It is a good idea. I had some writers at various points whom I wish I had educated on the matter; but hindsight is always 20/20.

Publicity materials definitely have a place in a music critic's life. The key is working out how to use them to your advantage—rather than relying on them wholesale.

PRO-TIP #2
Get the Words Right

You would imagine that using the correct words is important for writing well. In its larger sense, however, it also includes avoiding rhetoric, avoiding clichés, and relying on verbose description.

One of the key literary critics and philosophers of the past, Eugenio Montale, did this beautifully. He talked about his target work in a straightforward and unpretentious manner, without wasting his time or energy in composing elaborately rhetorical tracts.

What this ought to say to you is that you need to write simply, clearly, and straightforwardly. Write your story, write your argument, and do not baffle us with either bullshit or errors.

Things to avoid

There are some very simple things of which you can steer clear, to help clean up your writing. These are:

strings of adjectives

long ways around saying what you mean

using words of which you aren't 100% sure of the meaning incomplete
   sentences.

A string of adjectives is not a review

You may be wondering what I mean by the statement provided above. What I mean is that making up strings of adjectives and adverbs to provide the body of your review, and by which to explain an album's greatness or otherwise, is meaningless. Why? Because it tells me absolutely nothing of value.

The worst thing is that such reviews are rarely written in full sentences. They don't provide the reader with a comfortable, or easy, reading experience in the basic (lack-of-full-sentence) construction; and nor does jumping over six adjectives and adverbs in a row make for a relaxing read.

Here is an excerpt from a review by a person who used to write for me:

> ...a wild '80s lick, sped to fuck, twisted-into-the-contrasting-thrash onslaught...

What does 'sped to fuck' actually mean? Fucking fast, maybe.

What does 'twisted-into-the-contrasting-thrash onslaught' mean? Nothing.

What is twisted into the thrash? And why is the thrash a contrast? And what is it contrasted against??

Here's another example:

> ...opens like a cigarette to the skin and burns til the stub...

With this one I'm going to be really pedantic and say that 'a cigarette to the skin' doesn't open: it doesn't open the cigarette and it sure as hell doesn't open the skin. It burns. That's all. It doesn't open and then burn; it burns the whole time.

Of course you could argue that both of these examples have meaning in a particular way; the first gives you a vague idea that the music is metal in a wild 80s, thrashy way. But it doesn't tell you what is twisted into the thrash, or what the thrash contrasts with. 'Onslaught' tells you that it's fairly full-on —and it's a word I only ever reserve for killer releases because of its implications.

However, the second statement is absolutely meaningless in every sense, apart from the notion of intensity. But it doesn't tell you anything about the music that explains why it is intense, nor why it is *burningly* intense.

I know that certain printed metal mags have pioneered this style of writing, but, regardless, it's poor writing. All music writers require a keen ear, a good eye, a sense of logic and rationality, and the ability to hear what works and what doesn't.

Above all, good writers are possessed of the ability to explain *why*. Nonsense sentences just don't work. I don't care if you write for *Terrorizer*: if you can't write well, and write an effective argument, then you need help!

The reason why both issues outlined above are critical issues is simple: these problems stop a writer from developing. Without a sense of what reads well, one can never write well. It also places concrete-like boundaries on your ability to express the ways in which an album works, from an informed perspective. One could argue that lots of adjectives demonstrates a broad vocabulary; I would argue that a broad vocabulary is absolutely useless to you if you have no idea of how to use it. Adjectives, in whatever style or form of writing you produce, do not illustrate an ability to make use of a language. All it illustrates is an ability to use a thesaurus.

As with a sense of critique underpinning your work, the words that you use help you to craft an insightful review. Without the ability to see both of these elements, one will never be able to develop into a writer of touching prose, and will only ever reach a low standard of production. Knowing the elements of good critique enables you to recognise many more things: the production, the mix, the artwork, the entire package, how a band has emerged from its roots (or gone back to them), and so on and so forth. Discovering a world beyond adjectives enables you to write with real feeling, and real meaning.

Beyond the land of adjective-thickened writing, the world is your oyster. You will have the literary flexibility to reach much greater heights: a vocabulary that you can use with ease, to achieve your desired effects easily (without stringing meaningless phrases together), and many more elements of critique to draw on in order to achieve (and display) true insight.

Words and punctuation that cause trouble

Many people—including native English speakers—can't get words and phrases right. Those who learn English as a second language are a little more astute, in my experience, about getting things right. Regardless of the status of your Englishes, if you can get some of the basics right, then you will save your editor a shitload of angst.

There is absolutely nothing more tedious than having to change the same words every day, simply because of poor usage or spelling on a writer's behalf. While it's not easy for a lot of people to get these types of things right, hopefully this will help!

1980s, 1990s, not 1980's or 1990's. You are using a plural, so leave the apostrophe out before the 's'. This goes for shorter forms too: 80s, 90s.

are (plural), *e.g.* there are a few moments (note the 'agreement' between 'are' and 'a few moments'—that's what to look for! If there is more than one, use 'are')

CDs, not CD's. You are using a plural, so leave the apostrophe out before the 's'.

Definitely, not definately—it helps to think of it as de-finitely: something finite is absolute—so is a 'definite' something

is (singular), *e.g.* the band is

its (possessive), e.g. the album is fresh, its artwork is shiny

it's (contraction for 'it is'), *e.g.* the band loves Estonia, it's heading back next year

style or **styles**, not styling or stylings

their (possessive), *e.g.* their guitars

there (position), *e.g.* it's over there

they're (contraction for 'they are'), *e.g.* they're brilliant songs

About pronouns

If you are talking about a band, you must remember that **a band** is **a thing**. While it is comprised of people, you can't use 'who', 'whom', 'they', etc when you write about it—you must use 'it'. The band has done this, and it has done that, NOT The band have done this, and they have done that. It is when you start talking about band members that you can write about them using pronouns like 'who': the band members, they have done this—and so on.

About punctuation

Commas (,)—make sure you always have matching commas in a side comment or parenthetical statement. *e.g.* The band, which has been around for 20 years, still has it.

Slashes (/)—aren't surrounded by any white space. Make sure you close it up. Such as: *and/or*, not *and / or*.

Basic writing tips

Make sure you use proper sentences! Running phrases over five or six lines (or a whole paragraph) is one massive fail. Split your sentences up, rephrase things until you have something snappy and direct. You need to use proper sentences in every single thing you write, from reviews to Q & A interviews. If you don't, you let yourself down.

Not only will your editor thank you, but so will your readers. It's incredibly difficult to read a sentence that goes on, and on, and on. For those of you who are grammar nuts, remember that a sentence (at its most elemental) is comprised of a noun (or subject) and a verb (action); e.g. Satan wept.

Proofread your work. If you have a phrase, such as 'at times' written early in the sentence, as well as later in the same sentence, take one of them out! Repetition can be effective if you use it well—but such repetition as that is not cool. It just appears poorly written.

Always use the style guide you're provided. If your editor says band names in bold and album and song titles in italics, do it. It shows you listen. Jumbling a string of adjectives together does not a review make. And as with much of life, the happier you make your editor, the better the opportunities you shall receive.

PRO-TIP #3

Tell a Good Story

All writers, regardless of creed, are storytellers. When your art form is words, you have a drive, however slight, to affect people. The type of affect differs between writers. Some writers want to move people emotionally; some want to drive people to buy things; some want to make people think, consider, or wonder.

Investigative journalists and news-desk journalists all tell stories. They tell stories about what is going on in the world (this type of person did this type of thing, with this result); or they tell stories (for example) about this person who battles with depression and this is how they've gotten through thirty years with their family intact.

Music journalists also tell stories. They tell stories about an album, how it affects them, the place it's likely to have in their life, and where they understand it to sit in genres, discographies, and rotations. They tell stories about festivals, people getting drunk at shows, bands getting audiences to create circle pits so large you can't avoid them. They tell stories about journeys through recordings and tours, about bands.

All of the foregoing tells you that even if you are not writing fiction, you are still a storyteller. And if I think back to the best music writers I've ever read, all of them have crafted a story. These stories were populated with characters (whether people or music characters), they had some sort of action (real or imagined), they had a conclusion or outcome. They were well-written, simple, and engaging.

The art of storytelling is what separates reviewers and talented critics. It is what gets some writers repeat gigs, and denies others any gigs at all. It is far more difficult to craft a good, engaging piece of prose, than it is to throw some meaningless adjectives together enthusiastically.

To move your writing into a higher realm, you need to learn to craft story. All stories have: a sense of argument and structure (start—middle—end, for example); characters (whether the 'character' is a person, or a thing, or a concept; action (effect or affect, events, journeys).

You will sometimes need to think rather abstractly to turn your review into a 'story', and you may need to rethink how you approach the term 'story' in the first place. All of those writers out there who manage to do it occasionally know that they strike gold when they do. The trick is learning to identify what you did, and learning how to replicate it; and then learn to replicate it consistently.

Music journalism might seem like the strangest place in the world in which to write a story. But it is perhaps one of the most logical. If you refer back to your ethnography, you are a participant, and an observer, and you are writing stories about your experience. If you refer back to the first Pro Tip and re-read rhetoric, you know that your stories can be persuasive tools.

Combining your ethnography and the principles of rhetoric with the basics of story writing is a very powerful position from which to create work. Each element is essential to a good writer/storyteller, and gradually learning to compose, rewrite, and revisit with these in mind will move your writing in the right direction.

PRO-TIP #4

Manage Your Workload

While this chapter is aimed more at editors than it is at writers, people in both camps may get something out of it. It's all about managing your workload, which, as an editor without guidance is really tough; and as a newbie writer is equally difficult.

Many music editors fall into the role, and very often do so without hand-overs, without guidance, without tips of any kind. What they learn, they learn the hard way. Hopefully this material will help you to get back on top, and broaden your vision back up to the big picture—which, realistically, is where you need to be focusing.

1. Sort out the promos on your desk

Most editors have piles and piles of promos, both digital and hardcopy. Allowing these to pile up, without a sense of organisation, is disastrous for your mental state. Here is one way of recognising what you can actually work with.

Categorise your promos

Sort them out into bands that you are familiar with, bands that you are not familiar with but have heard of, and bands that you do not know from a bar of soap.

For bands you are not familiar with, set aside some time to go through Encyclopaedia Metallum online to determine genre.

Now, sort all promos by genre.

Focus on the genres that you know you will not hate outright, and disregard the remainder. If there are any genres from the Metallum listings that are vague, give them a listen before you determine whether or not to disregard them.

For writers: There is no point reviewing material that you will not be fair to. And for editors: do not include material that does not support your publication's purpose, focus, or audience, unless you have a very good reason for doing so.

2. Determine expectations

Labels will tell you that you ought to review everything, and that you could probably try to move heaven and earth to do it. Publicists who deal with labels on your behalf will say the same thing, but will also take anything that you can provide.

For a label publicist, all publicity is good publicity. If you can only do one promo off a label in a given month, they will take what they can get.

Obviously, as writers and workers we expect to be able to get through as much as we are given. Heads-up: It is simply not realistic.

Publicity guys will often say that they think a writer can do one review per day. Or even two or three. I have had that myself. The reality of critique is that it is simply not enough time to absorb an album. If you have a formula, then yes you can do it. So unless you work a month behind all the time (which is better than nothing), you can listen to 30 albums on rotation for a month, then write about them while you're listening to the next 30.

You can do it, but it is goddamn awful.

As an editor, I expected one review from my writers every three days. I think that is more than enough: one day to listen, one day to write, one day to listen/review. Obviously this is not ideal for the majority of albums, but in the working sense of a professional publication, it is fair to the writer, to the publication, and to the labels that feed you with material.

3. Determine your reporting timeframe… and stick to it

All publications (or editors, and freelance writers) have a responsibility to report back to labels or publicists on material that they have reviewed. It is not just good manners, it's a matter of professionalism; because in return, publicists have to report to bands and labels on their activity.

The best way to do this is establish a monthly cycle. Keep links to your writers' work throughout the month, and report on them to all publicists on or before the end of the month. If you report on the 1st of every month on activity for the foregoing month, that would work too.

The side-benefit of sticking to your reporting timeline is that it forces you to prioritise the material that you are going to work with.

For example, if I have a month, I sort the work like this:

1. material suitable for the publication
2. material from point (1) for which I have writers I know will be fair (i.e. not gushingly stupid, and not scathingly horrid, without reason)
3. material that has an accompanying interview opportunity
4. material that has an accompanying event review opportunity
5. everything else.

Albums that come parcelled with interview or gig review opportunities should always take precedence. This is because you get more bang for your buck (two or three pieces from the one item, potentially creating one or two super-knowledgeable writers), and it makes publicists happy: album promo opportunity x 3, gig promo x 3.

If you're an independent writer or blogger, and you get promos via something like Haulix, put your reviews into Haulix, and use their rating systems. As a back-up you can email the label, but at least on Haulix you also have a history of your reviews.

4. Something is better than nothing

Given point (2) above, you have the call as to how long the reviews are that you provide. If you are only given the space to allow your writers 150 words, then that's all you can do. If you have the space for pages and pages, then you're lucky!

Never worry about what labels and publicists want. You have to act in the best interests of your publication (as an editor) and yourself (as a writer). If you start doing exactly what the industry want you to do, then all your independence dissipates instantly.

Besides, practising saying 'no' is beneficial. It helps you manage your workload more effectively, and it helps the industry to respect you, because people gradually find out you can't be pushed around. Not being a pushover in this industry is hard work, and, as always, extremely useful.

PRO-TIP #5

Harsh Editing is Always Justified

Having edited others' work (not just music journos but also writers of textbooks, memoirs, and theses) for a more than 10 years, I'm a little bit inured to harshly editing people. I do it because it needs to be done. Harsh editing is always justified.

In terms of young reviewers, and those who want to get somewhere in the industry, harsh editing is not simply justified; it is essential.

Editing, done right, accomplishes all of the following:

- it maintains the quality of your publication
- it teaches writers what they can not (and will not) get away with if they want to write for you
- it teaches writers how to improve their work, and why
- it creates consistency across a publication, unmarred by poor writing or stupid errors
- it creates a publication's family, based on respect and increasing knowledge.

Good editors will take a number of different approaches, but they all come down to bluntness, tempered with diplomacy, and a lot of explanation.

In my experience, this method tends to help a writer over his or her hurdle. It also enables him or her to develop, because it provides the flexible, explanatory environment in which questions can be asked, ideas bounced, and new ideas created.

Many writers, especially young writers, are so keen to please that any form of directness causes them to get sad, or lose heart, or whatever. That's where your diplomacy skills are essential: you need to be able to walk your writers through this (potentially volatile) territory, and come out good friends at the end.

While I understand the 'let's all take it personally' reaction among writers (having been an edited writer myself, and having been at the harsh end of the stick no less), my internal, very personal response to it—which my writers never hear—is *harden the fuck up*. You write for a professional publication, expect to get treated like a professional writer.

Professional writers cop a whole lot on the chin. They are told in no uncertain terms what is wrong with their work, and they use this information as a means of improving what they do. A professional writer will only make a mistake once. Good editors make sure that young writers (in particular) do not make a mistake more than twice. And outstanding editors of music writers will develop every writer in some way, shape, or form.

When I am in an editorial role (and this is true for my past roles), if I have to work with a writer three times on the same issue, I give up and I look elsewhere for another writer. Because, clearly, this person is not learning quickly enough to keep pace.

My standard rule is 'three times is enough', especially when I have a lot to do, a huge list of releases to get through, a large team, and I have spent significant hours (usually into the early hours of the morning, via email) speaking with contributors about the hows, whys and wherefores.

As an editor, you can never apologise for editing your writers' work. It is your job. The quality of the work in a publication (online or printed) comes down to your intervention. A publication is only as good as its editor, and if its editor can't spell, or help a writer to craft a story, then the whole lot will be a mish-mash of haphazard works.

If you don't agree with what your writer has produced—regardless of whether it is good or not—and you know that your readership is going to react, always ask the writer if he or she is sure that's what they want published. Tell them what the likely reaction is going to be. If you get a yes, publish it; and then afterwards do not take the work down (if it's online) or recant it (if it's in print). Writers need to learn to be responsible for their opinions, and good critics will always publish what they *intend* to publish.

Happily, my method seems to work. It appears rather crude and unforgiving, written out like this. But sometimes people need to know what goes on, what an editor of a music mag is thinking, and how that editor works (and why).

If you are an editor yourself, never be afraid to tell people these things because it's through information that people gain understanding.

CONCLUSION

Falling into music journalism is easy. It is, in this day of the internet, possibly one of the easiest things to 'fall' into, if you have an interest in music, and an interest in writing. You can start a blog, write for someone else's blog, hook up with an online magazine... and start writing.

If you're persistent, you'll get more gigs. If you're prolific, you'll get even more gigs and opportunities. If you have even a slight talent for writing, you'll become a natural leader (eventually). It's a curious culture, because you don't even need to know what you are doing, in order to get gigs.

Most of these gigs aren't paid. You get the CD (or DVD), or entry to a show, as compensation for your work. But that's ok. I did that for many, many years, even as the key metal writer for a number of publications.

But what this book has demonstrated, is that you can never really shine as a music critic if you don't pay attention to ethnography, critical principles, and storytelling. You can review, but not be a critic. You can write, but not tell a story. You can edit, but not mentor writers.

And you can do all of the above, without even knowing what constitutes good writing.

Hopefully this book has taken you through some material that will help you to develop as a writer. It has been based on years of writing, mentoring writers, and analysing the process in order to come up with the hows, whys, and wherefores of this type of work.

If this book is the first that you've really read on the topic, with a bit of luck it will inspire you to read more, in different areas of critique, to discover essays on the topic. Hopefully you will gain an appreciation for how hard it is to do your job well, and how satisfying it is to nail it and gain appreciation from your peers for what you do.

More importantly, I hope that this book has inspired you to work hard, read broadly, and give you a solid footing to build on with future learning.

We live in an age where producing reviews, features, interviews is easy. You don't need to struggle for readership like you did 20 years ago. You are competing with others, sure! But are you competing with people who review and fell into the industry? Or are you competing with people at a higher level than yourself?

Regardless of whether or not you have the luxury of working with a talented editor, one whose focus is on writer development, and one with a fine appreciation for criticism, you can ensure that you grow in this field. It takes longer, and is a harder road, when you do it on your own. But if even one thing from this book helps you to do that, then my job is done.

Lifelong learning is important, and writers so often neglect their own development. It's an incredibly positive frame of mind to get into, though, and when you start to read, write, and learn, you find that many more pathways are open to you. Formal learning is not particularly necessary; effective reflection, and a willingness to learn, are the best ways of ensuring you don't get stuck amongst the 'establishment'.

APPENDIX

QUICK REFERENCE GUIDES

Each of the Quick Reference Guides in this section is short, sharp, and shiny. The Guides provide key reference points of the major ideas in each of the more lengthy chapters of the book, so that you can use them as a references long into the future.

Quick Reference Guide To:

ALBUM REVIEWS
& CRITIQUE

1. Listen to the album as though it stands alone. It is a singular recording, in a singular instance, of a particular genre.

2. While you listen, take into consideration the lyrics, the artwork, the construction.

3. Listen to the album a second time and write down everything you hate about it.

4. Listen to the album a third time and write down everything you love about it.

5. Compare your two lists.

6. Make more notes about how the album made you feel, what its production was like, what would improve it, does it fit its genre, etc.

7. Structure your notes so you have a mini-essay, a story, a way to engage your audience.

Quick Reference Guide To:

THE INTERVIEW

1. Prepare, prepare, prepare. Read as much as you can: other interviews, reviews, historical notes, liner notes, whatever you can find. Keep good notes.

2. Pull your notes into interview questions, as many as you can write.

3. Refine your list into 10 questions. Give them some structure and style, so your feature will be easier to write.

4. Print your questions out.

5. Know the time of your interview, and who is calling whom.

6. Make sure your technology works. Test it! Twice!

7. Relax, smile, and use your "best" voice.

8. Engage in small talk, let your interviewee talk, but be mindful of the time.

9. If you strike Mr Business, make him laugh.

10. Follow the conversation, and check off your questions in pencil as you go.

11. Thank your interviewee before you hang up.

Quick Reference Guide To:

THE EMAILER

1. Prepare, prepare, prepare (see the QRG to the Interview)

2. Pull your notes into interview questions, as many as you can write.

3. Refine your list into 10 questions.

4. Make sure each question is just one question. Add a contextual sentence to the start of it if you feel it would be easier to respond to.

5. Split multi-part questions into two separate questions

6. Remove any question to which could be answered simply 'yes' or 'no'

7. Keep your questions focused

8. Keep your language very simple; can each one be answered without having to be clarified?

9. Check them over fifty million times until you're happy with them

10. Remove any obstacles to reading; this is important for people who speak English as a second language.

Quick Reference Guide To:

THE FEATURE ARTICLE

1. Transcribe your interview

2. Paraphrase to create prose

3. One sentence between quotes does not make a feature article

4. Remember you are writing a story

5. Your article should have a natural sense of rhythm and flow

6. Restructuring quotes is acceptable

7. Be careful of making assumptions

8. Think it's finished? Let it sit overnight.

9. Read it aloud on Day 2, tweak until you're happy.

10. Go back and write an engaging, summarising introduction.

Quick Reference Guide To:

THE Q & A PIECE

1. Transcribe your interview
2. Restructure it for sense and natural flow
3. Work to the Rule of Thirds: your Q & A is still a story!
4. Write yourself out as much as possible
5. Remember that spelling, punctuation, and complete sentences are still important.
6. Think it's finished? Let it sit overnight.
7. Read it aloud on Day 2, tweak until you're happy.
8. Go back and write an engaging, summarising introduction.

REFERENCES

1. "Ethnography" at Wikipedia. Online. URL: [http://en.wikipedia.org/wiki/Ethnography]. Last updated: unknown. Last accessed: 8 April 2012.

2. http://www.cs.nott.ac.uk/~tar/DBC/dbc-lecture4.pdf. Last updated: unknown. Last accessed: 8 April 2012.

3. "Virtual Ethnography" at Wikipedia. Online. URL: [http://en.wikipedia.org/wiki/Virtual_ethnography]. Last updated: unknown. Last accessed: 8 April 2012.

4. Ravelli, Louise. 2004. Continuum Publishing Group: London.

5. "Metal: A Headbanger's Journey" at Wikipedia. Online. URL: [http://en.wikipedia.org/wiki/index.html?curid=5514346]. Last updated: unknown. Last accessed: 8 April 2012.

6. Goodall, H. Lloyd. 2000. Alta Mira Press: Maryland USA.

7. "Participant Observation" at Wikipedia. Online. URL: [http://en.wikipedia.org/wiki/Participant_observation]. Last updated: unknown. Last accessed: 8 April 2012.

8. Goodall, H. Lloyd. 2000. Alta Mira Press: Maryland USA. Page 10.

9. This lecture is available at http://www.cs.nott.ac.uk/~tar/DBC/dbc-lecture4.pdf. Last updated: unknown. Last accessed: 8 April 2012.

10. "Critic" at Wikipedia. Online. URL: [http://en.wikipedia.org/wiki/Critic]. Last updated: unknown. Last accessed: 8 April 2012.

11. AICSA Member Profile: Myk Mykyta. Online. URL:

[http://www.aicsa.net.au/profile/members/006.html]. Last updated: unknown. Last accessed: 8 April 2012.

12. http://www.aicsa.net.au/profile/members/006.html. Last updated:

13. "Eugenio Montale" at Wikipedia. Online. URL: [http://en.wikipedia.org/wiki/Eugenio_Montale]. Last updated: unknown. Last accessed: 8 April 2012.

14. "Montale, Eugenio 1896-". Online. URL: [http://www.enotes.com/eugenio-montale-criticism/montale-eugenio-vol-7]. Last updated: unknown. Last accessed: 8 April 2012.

15. ibid.

16. Definition of 'critique' from the Oxford American Dictionary.

17. 'Criticism' at Wikipedia. Online. URL: [http://en.wikipedia.org/wiki/criticism]. Last updated: unknown. Last accessed: 9 May 2012.

18. 'Film Criticism' at Wikipedia. Online. URL: [http://en.wikipedia.org/wiki/Film_criticism]. Last updated: unknown. Last accessed: 9 May 2012.

19. James, Clive. 'A Death in Life' from Snakecharmers in Texas. 1989. Picador Books: New York.

20. 'One Sheet' at Wikipedia. Online. URL: [http://en.wikipedia.org/wiki/One_sheet]. Last updated: unknown. Last accessed: 9 September 2012.

ABOUT THE AUTHOR

Leticia is a 30-something blogger based in Adelaide, South Australia. She writes music criticism, character fiction, essays and screenplays; blogs about the music industry and metal in general; and loves good friends, good life, and good beer. You can read her music journalism work at www.biodagar.com

Leticia's History in Music Journalism
I started writing music journalism while I was at uni, for the UniSA paper *Entropy*. After I left uni, I was headhunted by my former editor (and live music photographic extraordinaire) Rod Magazinovic, to write for him for the online magFasterLouder, which I did for several years. During this time I cut my teeth on some fantastic interviews (my first ever proper interview was with the almighty Rob Halford) and really started to build a bit of a profile. When FasterLouder cut back on their metal publishing, I started looking elsewhere... and eventually produced my own magazine, Metal as Fuck.

Metal as Fuck This was my proudest achievement, and even after I closed the publishing house I continued to produce and edit it. By our second year, we had thousands of followers on Twitter, and hundreds and hundreds of fans on Facebook, and had started gaining some really positive press both locally and internationally.

By early 2011, needing a change of direction (i.e. time to relax), I got a real job and sold Metal as Fuck to Radar Media, who now run the 'zine with aplomb.

Many of my writers and photographers I adore. I feel really privileged to have worked with so many beautiful, wonderful, talented people worldwide. Few people get an experience like it. I was recognised for this work in 2012, when I was interviewed by Canada Arts Connect for *Girls Don't Like Metal*.

CPSIA information can be obtained at www.ICGtesting.com
Printed in the USA
LVOW11s1522301015

460445LV00006B/513/P

9 780992 283704